A CREATIVE STEP-BY-STEP GUIDE TO

CLIMBERS
AND TRELLIS PLANTS

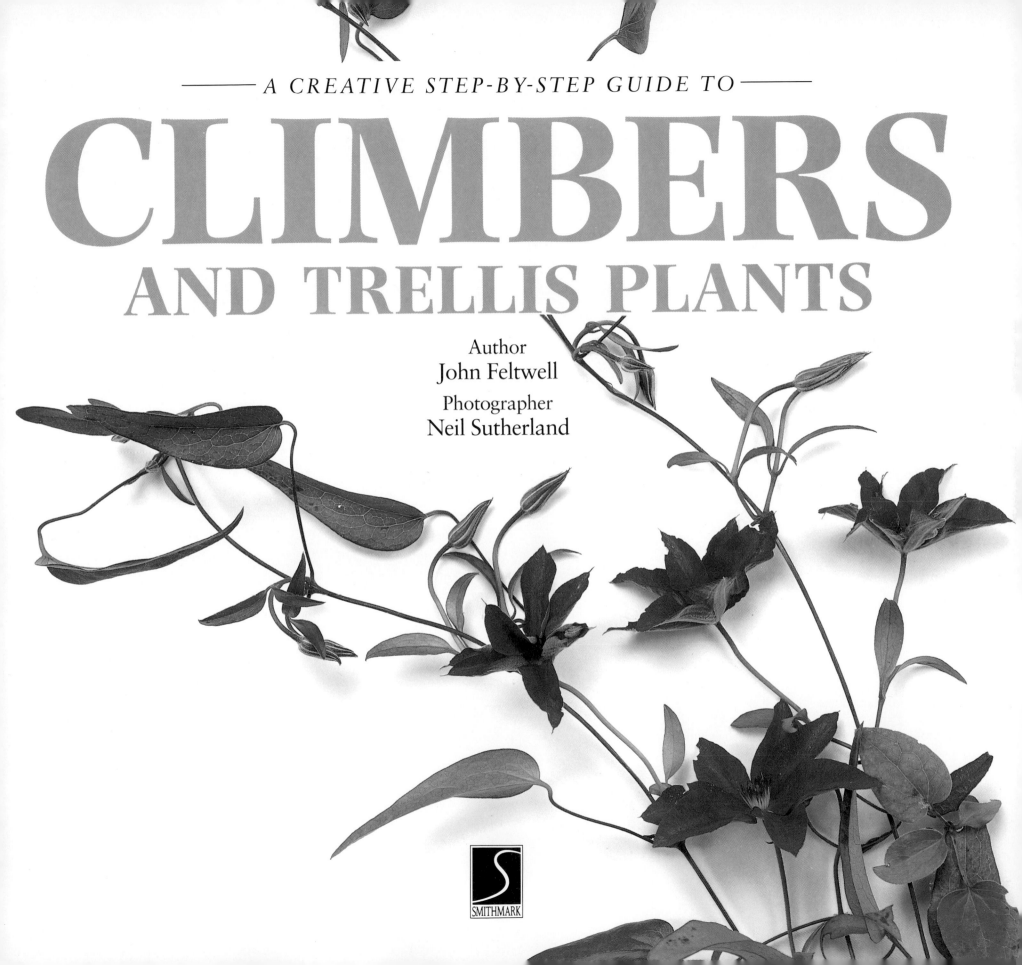

A CREATIVE STEP-BY-STEP GUIDE TO

CLIMBERS
AND TRELLIS PLANTS

Author
John Feltwell

Photographer
Neil Sutherland

SMITHMARK

CLB 4140

This edition published in 1996 by SMITHMARK Publishers, a division of U.S. Media Holdings, Inc., 16 East 32nd Street, New York NY 10016

SMITHMARK books are available for bulk purchase for sales promotion and premium use. For details write or call the manager of special sales, SMITHMARK Publishers, Inc.16 East 32nd Street, New York, NY 10016; (212) 532-6600

Produced by CLB Publishing, Godalming Business Centre Woolsack Way, Godalming, Surrey, UK

ISBN 0-8317-7576-9

Printed in Singapore
10 9 8 7 6 5 4 3 2 1

Credits
Edited and designed: Ideas into Print
Photographs: Neil Sutherland
Typesetting: Ideas into Print and Ash Setting and Printing
Production Director: Gerald Hughes
Production: Ruth Arthur, Sally Connolly, Neil Randles, Karen Staff, Jonathan Tickner

THE AUTHOR
John Feltwell has written 30 illustrated books, covering gardening, conservation and natural history for children, and has acquired an international readership. He is also a professional photographer, the proprietor of Garden Matters Photo Library, and many of his photographs appear in this book. Dr. Feltwell trained as a zoologist and botanist and lectures at universities in the UK and USA. He lives in Sussex with his wife and two children and travels the world in search of gardens and garden plants to photograph and research.

THE PHOTOGRAPHER
Neil Sutherland has more than 25 years experience in a wide range of photographic fields, including still-life, portraiture, reportage, natural history, cookery, landscape and travel. His work has been published in countless books and magazines throughout the world.

Half-title page: Plant Hedera helix 'Goldheart' *in a sunny position to maintain its delightful variegated foliage.*
Title page: Clematis 'The President' *has a long flowering period that lasts all summer until the fall.*
Copyright page: The rambling rose 'Excelsa' and the miniature 'Pink Bells' make a superb show growing together on a fence and gate.

CONTENTS

Introduction

CLIMBING ASPIRATIONS

The motivation for growing a climbing plant often comes from seeing a stupendous specimen in a private or public garden and wanting to grow it at home. Today, with the increase in plant breeding and the advent of rapid distribution systems, the world's climbers and their horticulturally improved cultivars can be delivered to garden centers and nurseries, even to our doorsteps, by mail-order. We can try almost any plant we desire. But how do we know what to grow and where to grow it, and whether it will survive in our gardens and conservatories? We have all been tempted to buy that exciting plant only to find that it perishes in a few weeks. This book presents a wide selection of climbers and trellis plants and provides practical advice that will help everyone get the best from their displays. The plants featured range from the familiar world of clematis and roses to the tropical splendors of bougainvilleas and beaumontias. Here, too, are features on purely foliage climbers, many of which provide an extra bonus of dazzling seasonal tints. Of course, the support systems for climbing plants are an equally important aspect of vertical gardening and there has never been a wider choice of designs, finishes and colors in trellis panels, arches, pergolas and other elements of garden 'hardware'. So, with such a wide choice of plants and support systems, now is the time to turn climbing aspirations into stunning reality.

Left: Honeysuckle fills the garden with scent. **Right:** *The bold flowers of* Mandevilla rosea.

Diversity of climbers

There are thousands of climbing plants and their role in nature is to use other plants to clamber skywards, using twining stems, suckers or tendrils. There is even a strangler fig in the rainforest that, having germinated in the canopy, kills the tree it climbs down. Many climbers are woody and capable of enormous growth and it is this characteristic that we use to encourage them to cover walls and arches. Sadly, many of the very colorful climbers are frost-sensitive and will not grow outdoors in temperate areas. Rainforest climbers may be spectacular, but are only suitable for tropical or Mediterranean climates. However, there is also a world of opportunist climbers that can be grown as annuals or biennials and they will grow quickly and produce plenty of interesting foliage and vivid color.

Among the most popular and easy-to-grow climbers are clematis, roses and wisteria. Gardeners enjoy these and other hardy climbers as species or improved varieties.

Above: Clematis create big splashes of color. Here, the large-flowered, blue 'H.F. Young' and the white 'Marie Boisselot' cover the background completely with foliage and flowers.

Left: A combination of night temperatures and degree of exposure to sun and shade makes the difference between ordinary fall colors and spectacular ones in Vitis coignetiae.

Right: The bright flowers of morning glory, Ipomoea hederacea, *punctuate a background of uniform leaves. Morning glories, nasturtiums and passifloras are all easy to grow for summer displays of colorful flowers.*

Above: Deciduous wisterias are very hardy and vigorous. The slight touch of rose in the flowers of W. floribunda 'Rosea' adds a fresh alternative to the pure white or purple form.

Left: The variegated ivy Hedera canariensis 'Gloire de Marengo' *provides plenty of evergreen foliage if you want to cover a wall or combine it with another climber, such as a rose.*

Right: 'Blush Rambler', a small-flowered rambling rose. With a wide variety of flower color and shape, fruits and vigor, climbers and ramblers are superb garden plants.

How do climbing plants climb?

Climbers are appreciated both for their flowers and for their foliage effects, especially when they shroud a garden fixture or cover an unsightly object. Their success in providing the vertical element in garden design is achieved in a variety of ways, such as twisting and twining stems, or by using tendrils or tiny roots that arise from the stem called adventitious roots. Clematis are typical of species with twining leaf stems, but honeysuckles use just their twining stems to reach their destinations. Ivies have adventitious roots, while the splendidly colored Virginia creepers use adhesive pads at the end of tendrils. Sweet peas and morning glories use tendrils. All climbers need a support, and in the wild they use trees and shrubs or even other climbers. In the garden, you can provide trellis, netting, pillars, fencing, canes and posts, as well as other plant material. Climbers growing amongst climbers are a real delight. Whichever method climbers adopt, they will use it powerfully and flagrantly to get where they want to be - upwards into full sun or lighter shade. As a gardener, you can assist the various climbers to climb, firstly by providing support and then, in the case of stem twiners, by tying up each leading stem, thus helping it push relentlessly forwards. The rotating stem tips and tendrils thrown out as lassos need to find suitable support, which you can provide for them (see pages 16-21).

Below: A section of a passion flower bearing the coiled tendrils that cling onto any nearby support - usually the stems of the same plant.

Twining stems

In most climbing plants, such as Solanum (far left), the leading stem rotates as it grows in a clockwise direction, as viewed from above. However, the Akebia (left) twists anticlockwise. If plants are wound in the wrong direction they will not readjust and often die, rather than twist in a natural direction.

Tiny adventitious roots arise from the main stem. The stem grows on in the gaps between them.

Left: On this ivy, adventitious roots grip the surface tightly and can invade loose plaster-work, making it more powdery. They act as an anchor point, allowing the vigorous ivy stems to grow further on.

Below: Virginia creepers cling on by themselves, using tendrils that end in sticky discs or hooks. These also provide some cushioning and protection from wind.

Twisting tendrils and splayed out discs secure the plant to the surface. They soon cover a wall, but the plants lose their leaves in winter.

These woody stems have twined around each other to form a strong framework.

A knot of leaf tendrils shows that this clematis is not averse to twining around itself.

Left: In this clematis, several stems have formed a knot of vegetation, enabling other stems to climb further up. This is something that honeysuckles also do in their quest to climb higher.

Right: The twining stems of the Russian vine (Polygonum baldschuanicum) are very prolific. Make sure you plant it in spot where it will have plenty of space to spread itself out. A new plant will need heavy pruning in order to train it into the desired position.

15

Trellis options

Set in pots, fan-shaped trellis makes an excellent support for climbers. This one has a natural wood finish.

White and green trellis panels are best set against a contrasting background. Screwed on a wall they make stylish backdrops for climbers.

Square trellis looks good on top of a fence, or screwed onto walls, where climbers can twine through the spaces. Square trellis can be used horizontally or vertically.

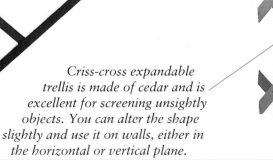

Criss-cross expandable trellis is made of cedar and is excellent for screening unsightly objects. You can alter the shape slightly and use it on walls, either in the horizontal or vertical plane.

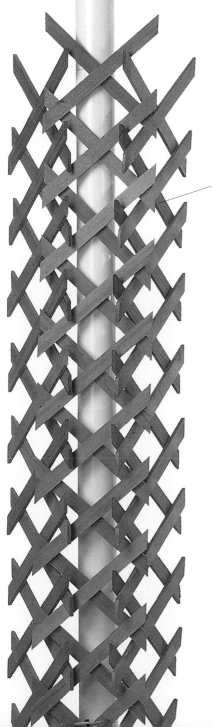

Tie three pieces of expanding trellis around a drainpipe to provide a support for a climber such as a clematis and hide the pipe from view. If the climber is growing in a pot on a patio, you can easily swap it for another plant to train up the trellis.

For a natural look that complements the plants trained onto them, you could try a woven-style trellis, such as this panel and the semicircular top section shown above. These are made of malleable willows and hazels and have irregular edges instead of the geometric outlines of more conventional panels.

Green trellis is a good choice for climbers that are to smother a wall or where you want a background that will not distract attention away from the plant. When covered with foliage, these panels help to enclose a green space.

Close-weave trellis is good for screening off small spaces and ideal for growing plants on. Tying up plants is easy and you can quickly achieve the effect you want from a climber.

Left: These large mesh, heavy duty panels are ideal for fixing to posts to create 'climbing partitions' in the garden. They can also be fixed directly to the wall.

Working with trellis

As we have seen on pages 16-17, trellis panels are available in a wide variety of styles and materials. Trellis framework is attractive by itself and its impact can be accentuated by painting it in different colors. Natural wood finish and white are favorite options, the latter conveying a 'classic' style to the garden. You can fix trellis panels to free-standing posts to create simple 'walls' that climbers can clothe with foliage and flowers, or you can build up arches, arbors, bowers and pergolas to suit your space and budget. In fact, you can buy many such trellis features as self-assembly kits, as demonstrated on pages 26-29. One of the main ways of using trellis panels is to fix them directly to a wall. You can do this simply by drilling through the battens and screwing directly into the brickwork. Do make sure that heavy panels are securely fixed and bear in mind that the climbers will add more weight to the structure. If you are using heavy duty, square mesh trellis you will need to decide whether to place the horizontal or vertical battens closest to the wall. One way might be better for the plants you use.

Below: The attractive diamond patterning of this wooden lattice is accentuated by the heavy battens used to make it. An ideal garden divider.

Above: A wooden trellis panel with the horizontal battens fixed directly to the wall. This leaves the vertical pieces free but plant growth may be restricted by the lack of space behind the cross pieces.

Above: Turn the panel round and the cross pieces form a series of 'rungs' on a ladder and are held away from the wall by the vertical battens. This might give climbers their best chance to develop.

Above: To save deciding which way round to fix the panel, you could simply space the whole thing away from the wall by fixing a suitable batten down the sides. This gives plants plenty of room.

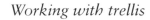

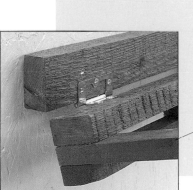

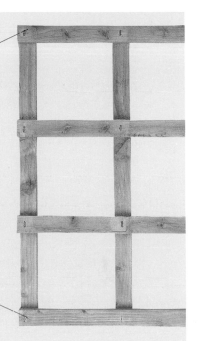

Fix a simple hook-and-eye catch here to secure the panel against the wall.

If you need to remove trellis panels to re-decorate the wall, why not hinge them as shown here? Fix them at least 24in (60cm) off the ground so that climbers can flex easily.

Hinge the panel to a batten so that it can swing down from the wall.

Above: *This small-mesh wooden trellis panel is very sturdy but also very heavy, so be sure to fix it securely. Ideal for a cosy bower.*

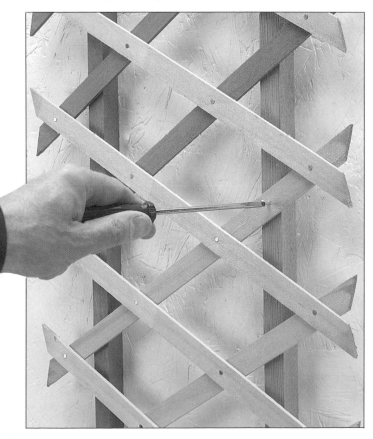

Left: *Expandable cedar trellis panels are usually quite thin and need support to work well. Try fixing cedar stakes to the wall and then screwing the panels directly to these. This will not only make the trellis more rigid but also create space behind.*

Right: *Curved trellis tops make attractive profiles in arches, arbors and pergolas. Combining curves and straight lines is very rewarding in garden design.*

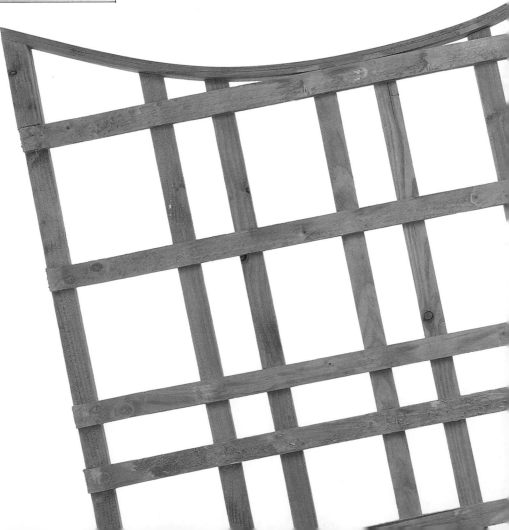

Climbing support systems for walls

Many climbers need plenty of support, otherwise they will produce a disappointing display. You can choose between a subtle but effective support system that will hardly be seen, or put in a larger system that then becomes part of your garden design. As we have seen, trellis panels are an effective support system and relatively easy to fix up. But what other options are available for supporting climbing plants against walls? Perhaps the simplest and cheapest plant support system is to use small nails or screws driven into the wall. These have straps or flexible tabs to support and guide the climbing stems as they grow; green plastic ones effectively disappear among the foliage. A more permanent system is an arrangement of wires stretched horizontally across a wall at about 12in(30cm) intervals. You can attach the wires to so-called 'vine eyes' driven or screwed into the brickwork. Remember to set this up before planting the climber. Such a system allows for all kinds of growth, whether it is a fan-shaped design or just a simple pillar of growth. There are various products available for tying plant stems to wire or trellis, from soft green string to plastic and paper ties. Always check that plants have not outgrown their ties each year and if using string check that this has not perished or broken. For scrambling plants, such as clematis, you can buy plastic netting in green, brown or white to match the plant or background.

You can nail these plastic spacers into the wall to allow air to circulate behind a trellis panel so that water does not collect and degrade the wood.

Nail these plant ties directly into bricks or mortar, wrap the long plastic tab around the climber and secure it. These ties can be adjusted and used many times.

These traditional style vine eyes can be driven directly into mortar. Thread wire through the small hole ('eye').

These substantial vine eyes can be screwed directly into wooden posts or into plugs inserted in brickwork.

Soft brown string may be less obtrusive than green string in certain situations, and will last one or two seasons.

Soft green string is ideal as a general-purpose 'camouflaged' material for tying up plants.

Small plant supports nailed into the wall close to leading stems encourage them to grow in the right direction and protect them from damage. Bend the soft metal tab over to secure each stem.

These plastic supports are easy to hide among the foliage of climbing plants. Nail them to walls or posts.

Using a vine eye

1 Hold the vine eye steady and hammer it firmly into the wall. Aim to allow a clearance of about 2in(5cm) between the eye and wall.

2 Pull the wire through the eye and twist it securely. You could use a threaded tensioning bolt to pull the wire taut between eyes.

Paper-covered wire 'twist-ties' are easy and convenient for 'light duties'. Also available in plastic.

Below: White plastic netting is the ideal support for the scrambling plant Plumbago auriculata. It is frost-sensitive and needs the warmth and shelter of this wall to thrive.

Garden wire is available in various thicknesses. This green, plastic-covered wire is thin enough to pass through vine eyes and strong enough to support plant growth. On walls, it blends in well with plants and flowers.

Being floppy, plastic clematis netting needs to be well secured all over, including the top and sides, to stop it falling down or blowing around.

Growing on walls

Walls are an obvious place to grow climbers, not least because they are ideal surfaces to fix trellis panels and wires. They represent the vertical element in gardens and offer many opportunities for display and experimentation. They are permanent structures that reflect heat and release it well after the sun sets, giving plants a longer growing day than elsewhere. Here is the place where gardeners in temperate climates can expect to get the best results from half-hardy or frost-sensitive species, or try a tropical favorite during the warm summer months. The aspect of the wall is important for some groups of plants, the majority of climbers enjoying walls that face the sun or are sideways onto the sun at its height. Consider the background color of the wall. White helps to accentuate plants and looks distinctive, but you may have your own ideas. If you are building a wall from scratch there are many bricks to choose, some in subtle colors that mellow with age. Your local stone is probably the best choice.

Above: *A wall clothed with glory vine* (Eccremocarpus scaber), *a native climber of South America that can reach 12ft(3.7m), and the striking ivy,* Hedera colchica *'Dentata Variegata'.*

Right: *The unusual* Dregea sinensis *is an attractive climber with delicate foliage and flowers, but must be grown against a warm wall in full sun. There is a variegated form available.*

Left: *The orange flowers of the trumpet vine, Campsis x tagliabuana 'Madame Galen', appear in late summer in huge sprays. This plant really benefits from the warmth and shelter of a wall.*

Below: *The cup-and-saucer vine (Cobaea scandens) bears many large, bell-shaped flowers from late summer. In temperate climates, it is best grown as an annual and will flourish in a warm spot against a wall.*

Wall shrubs

With a good support system of wire or trellis, a wide variety of scrambling, semi-climbing or partially ascending shrubs can be grown as climbers. These include ceanothus, pyracanthas, the striking marmalade bush, Streptosolen jamesonii and the widely grown Euonymus fortunei from China.

Left: *Heavy with bright berries, pyracanthas are ideal on walls.*

Below: *Ceanothus impressus will thrive if supported on a wall.*

Choosing a good plant

Choosing a suitable plant at a nursery or garden center need not be a gamble. Clearly, there are many factors that influence the future success of your plant, but you can eliminate some of these factors by buying from a reliable source and carefully examining the plant before you buy it. It should be healthy, sturdy and well-proportioned with, perhaps, plenty of leaf production, some flowers and new and developing buds. There should be no signs of damage or disease, no wilting or premature leaf, flower or bud loss. Compare the plant with adjacent specimens to see how they rate on these features - you can easily be deceived by apparent good looks. There might be even better specimens next door. Is the plant well-proportioned for the job you have in mind for your climber? Perhaps you need three or four lead shoots to train your plant. Feel the potting mixture to ensure that it is well-watered. Look to see whether the climber is potbound with too many roots or so frail that it falls out of the pot at the slightest touch. If the plant does not measure up to all these criteria, reject it and find another source of supply.

Sometimes, however, even though you follow all these guidelines, you still end up with a plant that does not perform well and this may be a feature of the plant's breeding or a variation caused by a genetic factor that cannot be identified by a close inspection. Furthermore, you may choose what seems to be an ideal specimen but its survival and success will depend on how you nurture it once you have planted it in the garden or conservatory.

A well-trained Bougainvillea *that has been encouraged to grow on two supports. It is flowering well and should thrive in the correct environment.*

This is a fine Mandevilla *specimen, sturdy and well-proportioned, with a keenness to flower.*

In a sheltered, sunny spot, mandevillas grow to about 12ft (3.7m) and flower in summer. Provide protection in winter in temperate climates.

It may be completely bare now, but this Wisteria *'Black Dragon'* has healthy shoots and strong buds that promise an eventual harvest of dark purple flowers in early summer.

Right: *Clematis wilt is caused by a fungus that can strike most of the plant or just a shoot or two. Cut it out as soon as you discover it and burn the diseased part. The plant should make a complete recovery.*

This winter-flowering Clematis cirrhosa *'Freckles'* has strong growth at the base and a good shape. This is more important than its height.

Ivies are robust plants and survive well in garden center containers. This is a good specimen of the Canary Island ivy, Hedera canariensis *'Gloire de Marengo'*.

Look for strong shoots and healthy foliage when buying honeysuckles. This is Lonicera japonica *'Halliana'*.

Containerized or bare root?

Above: *Pot-grown climbing or rambling roses should have a healthy root system and strong shoots. Best planted out in spring.*

Below: *Bare-rooted climbers are best planted out in the fall. This is a good, sturdy example, with three strong shoots.*

Above: *This close-up shows where the upper growth has been grafted onto the rootstock of Wisteria sinensis at the nursery, with the protective grafting wax still visible. Always choose grafted plants; seed-grown ones take many years to flower.*

Look for healthy root growth and fibrous roots, with no suckers.

25

Building a pergola

Self-assembly pergolas are available from garden centers and mail-order suppliers. Following the instructions, you should be able to put one together in just a few hours. The one featured on these pages has four uprights, two side beams, four cross beams and two trellis panels. The wood is treated with a preservative stain that will protect it from rotting and will not harm plants growing on it. When you have unpacked the kit and are ready to begin, it is a good idea to have someone to help you and you will also need a hammer, nails, gloves and a stepladder. Wear gloves to prevent splinters and as protection against the preservative stain applied to the wood. If you prefer to build a pergola from scratch, you can buy the wood and cut it to size at home. You will need to stain and preserve the wood as well. Naturally, this is a cheaper option than buying a ready-to-assemble kit. Whichever method you choose, you need to decide where to site the pergola and how to support the uprights. You could sink them in concrete or fix them to metal post holders driven into the ground. This last method require shorter uprights and, as they are not sunk into the ground, they will not rot.

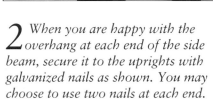

1 *Support two of the uprights and lower one of the un-notched side beams into the groove. Decide on the spacing of these uprights before securing them into the ground.*

2 *When you are happy with the overhang at each end of the side beam, secure it to the uprights with galvanized nails as shown. You may choose to use two nails at each end.*

Left: Bold lines dominate this part of the garden. This sturdy wooden pergola has four climbers planted around its base: clematis, wisteria, climbing potato and honeysuckle.

Right: Rope is used as a support on this pergola for the flowers and foliage of a striking climbing rose. Rope makes an attractive change from thin pieces of rustic wood, wire or twine.

3 Once the two sides of the pergola are complete, join them together by dropping in one of the four cross beams. Put the end ones 'outside' the uprights for a stable structure.

4 With the far end cross beam also in place, space the other two out equally. The width of the pergola is set by the notches in these cross beams.

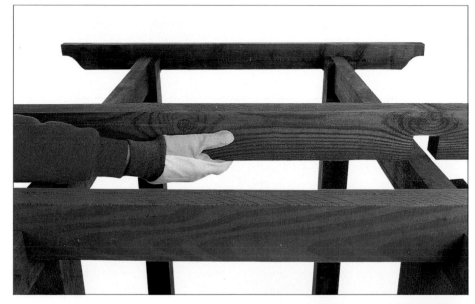

5 After checking that everything is aligned correctly, nail the cross beams in place directly to the top of the side beams. A single nail at each end should be enough to secure them.

6 Position the first trellis panel in between the uprights and nail it into place. Raise the panel about 6in(15cm) off the ground to protect it from soil moisture and rain splash.

7 With the second trellis panel in place opposite the first, the pergola is complete. This demonstration sequence has not included the vital task of fixing the uprights securely.

Check the base of the uprights regularly to ensure that the wood remains sound.

Building a rose arch

A rose arch can form a major feature in a garden and, not surprisingly in today's 'instant result' world, you can buy one as a flat-pack, complete with simple assembly instructions. The kit featured on these pages was delivered as four components - two side pieces and two roof sections - and it was very heavy. Before you begin work, it is vital to have someone available to help you and to equip yourself with a tape measure, hammer, nails, an adjustable wrench and a pair of stepladders. The first vital decisions to make are where to site the arch and how to support it in the ground. In this kit the uprights are long enough to sink directly in the ground, which you could set in concrete for stability. If the 'legs' are shorter, you could fit them into metal post holders sunk in soft ground or attach them to four bolt-down post sockets in a concrete base. The best way of assembling the kit is to do it at ground level, as the photographs show. You will certainly need help to move the completed arch into its final position. Such an arch can mark the change from one part of the garden to another or frame your main view from the house. Embellished with roses, honeysuckles, clematis and other climbing plants, even a simple trellis arch can quickly become a treasured focal point.

1 *First bolt the two roof sections together, using the supplied bolts. You may need to redrill the holes to make sure the bolts go through easily. Tighten up with a wrench.*

2 *Butt the sides of the arch up to the roof sections. There is a batten across each roof piece (technically known as a purlin) against which the top of each side will fit snugly.*

3 *Nail through the roof section into the uprights. Two nails on each side will increase the rigidity of the structure and help it bear the weight of climbing plants.*

This lozenge-shaped piece of wood forms a decorative finial to hide the join between the two roof sections.

Left: *This trellis rose arch forms a natural doorway into a different part of this cottage-style garden. A white climbing rose makes it way over the arch from the left to mingle with a honeysuckle planted at the right. Both will provide scent and color during the warm summer months.*

4 Check that the sides are parallel and measure how far they are apart. You will need to know this so that you can dig corresponding holes or locate post holders accurately.

5 The completed rose arch looks splendid partnered with two trellis panels. Even before it is clothed in climbing plants, the arch leads the eye into the next part of the garden.

Below: An iron framework draped with a vine creates this decorative arch. The arch is used in garden design, not only to show off plants and to attend to the 'vertical' aspect of gardening, but as an opportunity to change the mood of the garden when you enter another part.

Pergolas and arches

One of the advantages of arches and pergolas is that they can accommodate the rampant nature of climbers and ramblers, allowing you to appreciate just how they would perform in the wild and admire the beauty of their flowers at eye level. Arches show off the plants in a very restricted area, but pergolas allow you to make more of a display; you could plant more than one example of a single species or a variety of species on a long axis. (The word 'pergola' stems from the Latin term meaning 'projecting cover'.) The significance to the viewers is that they can pass through a pergola and experience the plants first hand, while the flowers on an arch or arbor are more of an inspirational delight. Pergolas and arches can make a great contribution to garden design. Both can be made of quite different materials, including wood, plastic, steel and brick, and both are available in self-assembly kits (see pages 26-29). There is something very attractive in the curves of an arch, especially when it frames a view through the garden, and if the arch is a tall one, it makes a big statement in the garden. If the arch is adorned with beautiful flowers, the embellished curve takes on even greater importance. Thinking about the contribution of curves and straight lines provided by pergolas and arches can encourage you to develop your garden design further.

Above: A floriferous climbing rose has taken advantage of this support. It is best to put in one plant on each side and allow them to meet in the middle, even though one might turn out to be more vigorous than the other.

Below: *This simple pergola has been embellished with very attractive trellis. a great foil on which to display a fine specimen of Clematis 'Ville de Lyon'.*

Right: *The combined flush of flowers of the wild climbing rose 'Seagull' flourishing on either side of an arch show off the true nature of the plant.*

Right: *This pergola has uprights made of brick, with wood cross beams. It is certainly very solid and will outlive an all-wood pergola. The advantage of brick piers is that they can support the colossal growth and weight of the vigorous wisteria that is planted on it.*

Planting a climbing rose

1 *Dig out a planting hole about 12in(30cm) across and deep. Make sure that the hole is at the center of the trellis and not to one side.*

2 *Dig over the base of the hole to aerate the soil and break it up to improve drainage. Add some rotted manure or other organic matter.*

3 *Fork the organic matter into the base of the hole below the plant where it will not reach the roots. Too much or too fresh manure may 'burn' the roots.*

The best time to plant a climbing rose is during the early fall or in the spring. Planting in early fall means that the plant has a few weeks in which to grow and establish itself before the onset of winter. Planting in the spring means that the plant gets off to a quick start and is likely to perform well. Bare-rooted roses tend to be hardier than containerized ones and are therefore better able to cope with the rigors of winter. Containerized roses are readily available from nurseries or garden centers and can be planted during the spring and early summer. On these pages we show how to plant a healthy, bare-rooted specimen that has been pruned back to its three main stems. Always stand a plant in water for at least ten minutes before planting. Once established, newly planted climbers and ramblers will need no pruning for at least two years. Simply remove the dead flowers. In later years, prune out spindly growth.

4 *Gently position the rose in the hole, taking care not to damage any roots, and arrange the roots evenly around the base of the hole.*

7 Spread out the branches of the climber and, even though they are short, tie in the shoots to the trellis using soft string and a simple knot.

5 Use a cane to check the planting depth. Fill in with the soil mixed with some peat or substitute, plus a slow-release fertilizer.

6 Firm the soil around the roots to eliminate air pockets. These can interfere with respiration of the roots, cause waterlogging and frost damage.

8 This well-proportioned climbing rose has every prospect of thriving from the good start it has been given. Water well until established.

Below: A superabundance of foliage and flower, all borne on long stems, bursts forth from this 'Pink Perpétue'. It was planted just a few months earlier.

Climbing roses

Roses are outstanding climbing plants, often displayed in prime positions on pillars, pergolas, trellises and walls. They prosper in a wide range of soils, although most roses prefer very slightly acid conditions, and need good drainage. If this is a problem, dig the soil over thoroughly and add plenty of well-rotted manure. In thin chalky soils, add more topsoil and work in manure. Once planted, roses require regular attention. Remove any suckers that emerge from below ground level, by pulling or cutting them out. In summer, tie in new growth, deadhead old blooms to encourage more flowers, hoe the soil to remove weeds and mulch around the base to suppress weeds and retain moisture. Apply a fertilizer according to the instructions and water the plants in dry spells. Spray against pests and diseases if necessary. In the fall, prune back most of the old flowering wood and secure the new shoots to their support to avoid winter storm damage. Burn prunings if possible to prevent the spread of disease.

Below: The magnificent Rosa banksia *performs best in a hot climate, where its long arching stems carry abundant pale yellow or white flowers. Double forms exist, too.*

Once the rose has been trained and secured to establish its arbor shape, prune it each year to keep it in check.

Below: Here growing on either side of a door, the rambler 'Bantry Bay' produces showers of semi-double pink flowers above its semi-glossy foliage. It grows to about 10ft(3m).

Above: It can be difficult to cram in masses of flowers into a small area, but rambling roses are the ideal solution. This arch is smothered in bloom during the summer months and forms a striking garden feature.

Left: 'American Pillar' rambles over pergolas and arbors with its showers of pale-eyed pink flowers. It is unscented and flowers only once, but is so vigorous and floriferous that it deserves its place in the garden.

Climbing and rambling roses

'Albertine', 'Aloha', 'Blush Rambler', 'Dortmund', Dublin Bay', 'Golden Showers', 'Guinée', 'Handel', 'Mme Alfred Carrière', 'Maigold', 'Mermaid', 'New Dawn', 'Paul's Scarlet', Rosa filipes 'Kiftsgate', 'Zéphirine Drouhin'

Climbing roses

Both ramblers and climbers make quality contributions to garden design, not only because they have large and abundant flowers, superb colors and, in some cases, scent and a habit of repeat-flowering, but because they add another dimension, both vertically and horizontally. Climbers tend to be extremely vigorous, reaching well up into the trees or over the house. They have sturdier stems, are more resistant to mildew and bear larger flowers and smaller flower trusses than ramblers. Some, such as the climbing China roses, or Bourbons, are repeat-flowering, whereas most ramblers flower only once. As ramblers are derived from hybrids, their spirit of adventure is generally diminished, but they can be encouraged to decorate walls, pillars, old tree stumps and trellis. They also perform well as weeping standards.

The differences in plant growth have an effect on how you prune climbers and ramblers. Climbers flower from old wood, which makes them easier to manage. They usually need no pruning. Ramblers flower from new growth, of which there is likely to be an abundance, and all old wood must be cut back to a suitable bud in winter. Encouraging a newly planted rose to cover a wall or trellis will occupy the mind while you consider which stems to cut out (or not). However, clearing out dead wood and any stems that cross each other will help to keep these decisions to a minimum.

Left: True to its status as a climber, the species rose, R. laevigata, *the Cherokee rose - a native of eastern United States and the state flower of Georgia - can grow out of control if not pruned back regularly. It enjoys the sun and has long stems covered in white flowers.*

Below: *An immaculately trained climber, Rosa 'Pompon de Paris' is skilfully displayed on this trellis. The stems bear uniform pink pompons, each one slightly raised up from the gray-green foliage.*

Above: *A delightful pair of scented roses - the white 'Alister Stella Gray' and 'Lawrence Johnston' - waft their perfume through the open window.*

Climbing and rambling roses

Generally speaking, rambling roses have pliable stems and will do better when trained against a firm support. The 'Blush Rambler' (above) is well proportioned, but needs to be pruned back to maintain this shape the following year.

Climbing roses have stouter, woody stems and need less support. Rosa 'Zéphirine Drouhin' (left) can be grown as a climber and pruned to shape. Here, it is intertwined with another climber, Clematis montana 'Alba'. It has the advantage of being thornless, as well as fragrant.

Smotherers for quick cover

Smotherers is a name given to certain climbers that are so vigorous that they tend to swamp everything they are attached to. Although many plants qualify for this description, two of those featured on these pages are particularly good examples: the so-called mile-a-minute, or Russian vine *(Polygonum baldschuanicum)*, and the coral vine *(Antigonon)*. The first is ideal for temperate climates, the second for warmer areas. Mile-a-minute is notorious for its prolific growth, hence its common name, but it has the advantage of flowering in the fall after many other climbers have finished. It is a member of the knotweed family, many members of which are weeds. The coral vine is a particularly effective smotherer and can be grown over an arbor. With such pretty strings of pink flowers, the plant has accumulated many common names apart from coral vine, including love vine, Mexican creeper (an indication of its wild origin), mountain rose and Confederate vine. The mass of vegetation produced by these smotherers can be left in place if it is not causing a nuisance or you can trim it back roughly to the required shape. It is easy to propagate both mile-a-minute and coral vines from seeds or cuttings.

In its own way, the glory vine *(Eccremocarpus scaber)* is also a smotherer. When fully established it covers walls and trellises with thickets of foliage. Its bright summer flowers are then followed by balloonlike pods.

Left: Eccremocarpus scaber, *the glory vine, from Chile has wands of attractive red-orange flowers; yellow- and redder-flowered cultivars are also available.*

Left: *The rose of montana, or coral vine* (Antigonon leptopus), *creates a breathtaking spectacle by forming this complete bower of foliage and flower over an arch.*

Left: The characteristic small leaves and long stems of Polygonum baldschuanicum *are clearly visible here. The stems also twist around themselves in their relentless race to cover as much distance as possible.*

Left: Mile-a-minute *hangs like a waterfall of vegetation from this trellis. Although the flowers are not exceedingly attractive individually, en masse they perform a great service as an effective screen.*

Clamberers with class

Colorful clamberers can make 15ft(4.5m) of growth annually, starting from seed at the beginning of the year. Nasturtiums, or more correctly tropaeolums, are excellent subjects, as they are energetic scramblers and climbers. As annuals, they produce flowers in late summer and fall, bringing a splash of color to the garden just when it is needed. A good range of tropaeolums is available, as there are at least 90 true species from South America, as well as many hybrids, some of which are herbaceous perennials. Nasturtiums are good at climbing trellis or shinning up other plants, scrambling up pillars or smothering the ground with their array of bright flowers. Try growing them over gravel between herbaceous beds. The dwarf forms can be grown as sprawling plants over the ground, thus creating attractive ground cover. When grown in pots or spilling from the top of walls, tropaeolums make good display plants, especially the variegated leaf types. A quite different and unusual climber is *Rhodochiton atrosanguineum*. It is frost-tender, but can be grown from seed during the spring and will thrive in well-drained soil in a sunny place. It bears distinctive red and dark purple flowers for many months during the warmth of summer.

Above: *Many tropaeolums can be grown equally well up pillars or in hanging baskets, their twining stems continually seeking purchase points. This is Tropaeolum majus.*

Right: *Here, tropaeolum has been encouraged to grow over a low arch from a bed of petunias, creating a foliage-rich but striking entrance to another area of the garden.*

Above: *When broken, the leaves and stems of nasturtium leak a whitish liquid that is a general insect deterrent. However, caterpillars of the cabbage white butterfly have a special interest in the leaves and can defoliate a whole display.*

Long leaf stalks carry the rounded nasturtium leaves well away from the main stem.

Right: Rhodochiton *climbs by twisting its leaf stalks around supports. It can be grown as a perennial for its evergreen leaves, but as it is sensitive to frost it is best treated as an annual in temperate regions.*

Below: The blooms of Rhodochiton atrosanguineum *are perfectly formed. As it develops, the center part of the flower extends to form a long trumpet.*

Above: Tropaeolum speciosum *is an extrovert climber, reaching 15ft(4.5m) from ground level in a season. The effect of a dark hedgerow smudged with the blood-red flowers is superb.*

Stylish wisteria

There are two widely grown wisteria species: *Wisteria sinensis* (Chinese wisteria) and *W. floribunda* (Japanese wisteria). They look very much the same and both are vigorous climbers that can reach up to 100ft (30m). The normal color form is pale lilac to purple, becoming paler as the flowers age, but in both species there are white - 'Alba' - forms. The large trusses of flowers, or panicles, make a fine spectacle, especially when they appear before the arrival of any young leaves. Wisterias blossom early in the year and sometimes again later at the end of summer. They produce a small amount of scent, but the flowers are always highly attractive to bumble-bees and other insects, some of which fall drowsily to the ground. Beware of these insects when constructing a pergola or archway that is to support a wisteria.

Growing wisteria is more a question of control than of nurture. They are mostly hardy and benefit from hard pruning after flowering and during the winter. They can damage gutters, pipework and roof tiles, as the twisting and turning lead shoots curl under anything on which to make a purchase. As they grow and enlarge, they may lift fittings away from the building.

Left: The massed ranks of panicles of Chinese wisteria, W. sinensis, *are captured at the moment in spring when the pergola and the plants it bears are in perfect harmony.*

Right: Not a leaf or leaflet is in sight on this magnificent mature wisteria, resplendent in its springtime blossom. In winter, when it loses all its leaves, wisteria can look quite unattractive.

Basic pruning

Wisteria is so vigorous that you may need to cut, or even saw, it back after flowering to keep it within bounds. At the end of the season, cut back smaller branches of new growth to just two leaves beyond the old woody stems, as here. A new shoot will arise from the leaf base.

The woody growth has a darker bark.

Above: At close range, the panicles are made up of pealike flowers, confirming wisteria as a member of the pea family, the Leguminosae.

Above: Chinese wisteria, Wisteria sinensis *'Alba'*, bears a mass of white, powerfully scented flowers in early summer.

Right: With its huge panicles dipping into the water, Wisteria floribunda *var.* macrobotrys *makes a bold statement in the garden - doubly so, when it is mirrored in the water.*

43

Clematis - the montana types

Montanas are very popular subjects that look terrific when they are in full bloom in the spring. Their flowers are small and borne prolifically all over the plant, often making a complete spread of color. In fact, clematis flowers are not flowers in the conventional sense, since the petals have been lost and the bright colors of the 'flowers' are really sepals and, in some cases, stamens. The basic color of the flowers of *Clematis montana* is snow white, but there are many other varieties ranging from pale to deep pink, and the size of the flowers varies, too. The scent of C. *montana* is retained in some of the varieties, varying from the vanilla of the true montana species to hot chocolate in C. *montana wilsonii*.

Clematis montana can be grown in most soils and in most aspects, but as an ornamental, the best way to show off its magnificent color effects is to grow it as a pillar, either on a specially made structure or trained up an old tree stump. Alternatively, if there is a garden structure that needs to be screened, then C. *montana* will do the trick and smother it completely. Montanas are superb climbers and use their twining stems as a means of support. Once they have secured a hold, they build on this and produce woody stems that make their progress through their support that much more permanent and secure. These vigorous plants just need an annual shear after flowering has finished to keep them within limits.

Left: Clematis always look good scrambling through other plants, which is their habit in nature. This C. montana *is growing through a* Ceanothus. *With its long twining stems, the montana winds through plants and then thrusts out its flowers.*

Below: Here you can see just how vigorous the true Clematis montana *can be, especially when it is allowed to perform unhindered over a trellis.*

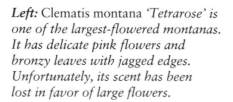

Left: Clematis montana 'Tetrarose' is one of the largest-flowered montanas. It has delicate pink flowers and bronzy leaves with jagged edges. Unfortunately, its scent has been lost in favor of large flowers.

Right: *With minimal cutting back, the entire mass of* C. montana *'Elizabeth' can be left in place on the trellis over the winter and will perform like this each year.*

Above: *Size, the arrangement of the flowers in four, and the leaflets - here a little jagged around the edges - are features that distinguish different montanas. This is* Clematis montana.

Right: C. montana *looks superb around the garden door. After a few years, a mature specimen will produce a bulk of old vegetation. Cut this back carefully to maintain its structure.*

Small-flowered clematis

There are about 300 different types of clematis to choose from, but here are a few of the smaller-flowered varieties, which have an array of delicate saucer-shaped flowers. You can choose from a huge range of colors to find one variety that suits your individual color scheme. Growing two or three varieties together adds extra interest and provides plenty of surprising color. These exciting colors and shapes are typical of many clematis, since their habit in the wild is to scramble through other vegetation, such as trees and bushes. Having used other plants for support, they then pop a flower on a long stem out of the tangle, where it will flower, be pollinated and produce fluffy seeds. This is the case with *Clematis alpina*, which scrambles through thickets and is similar in form to many of those shown on these pages. Alpinas flower in early spring. *Clematis viticella* also has small flowers and will bloom in shady as well as sunny positions. Viticellas and their hybrids are very vigorous and ideal for covering a shed or smothering a hedgerow. They can put on up to 20ft(6m) of growth in a year. Attractive hybrids include *C.v.* 'Purpurea Plena Elegans', 'Kermesina' and 'Voluceau'. They have the advantage of flowering in late summer and into the fall, when many other plants in the garden are past their best.

Alpinas - cultivated and uncultivated

Alpinas are accustomed to high altitudes and low temperatures, so it is not surprising that they are some of the first varieties to flower in the spring. In the wild, Clematis alpina is not as generous with the number of flowers produced on each plant, as can be seen from the photograph at left, taken in the Austrian Alps. Cultivated varieties sold under the same name can have five times this number and look superb, as in this 'Frances Rivis' at right.

Left: Clematis macropetala *is a very versatile species that will grow in both sunny and shady positions. It flowers in mid-season, producing delightful, purple-and-white, semi-double flowers.*

Right: Growing clematis through shrubs and up trees is simply pandering to their preferences in the wild. Here, C. v. *'Abundance' spills out of the shrub* Berberis x ottawensis *'Purpurea' to make a fine display.*

Left: Both the flowers and seeds of the summer-flowering Clematis integrifolia *'Rubra' can be seen on the plant at the same time. This herbaceous species grows to about 3ft(90cm).*

Orientalis and tangutica varieties

Two very vigorous climbers that have no difficulty in scrambling over walls to create masses of tiny, bell-shaped flowers are Clematis tangutica (above right), and Clematis orientalis 'Bill Mackenzie' (below right). They are so similar that they were once classified as varieties of each other. They are commonly known as orange peel clematises. Both produce fluffy seedheads that attract seed-eating birds to the garden.

Large-flowered clematis

There is no doubt that some of the largest and most magnificent flowers in any garden are those of the clematis. The large-flowered clematis varieties have flowers that are as big as dinner plates and they can make a spectacular feature in the garden. Late large-flowered clematis tend to be slightly smaller than early-flowering varieties, at about 6in(15cm) across. The sepals of the large-flowered cultivars are typically large, wide and sometimes floppy and, according to the cultivar, may be produced early in the season, mid-season or during late summer and fall. Generally speaking, large-flowered clematis are frost-hardy and well worth displaying on walls, trellises and pillars. They are tolerant of most aspects and, with the exception of many of the earlies, can be grown in full sun. In hotter climates, clematis tend to bloom with richer, warmer colors. There are also doubles and semi-doubles of large-flowered cultivars. If a double-flowered variety blooms for the second time in the year, the flowers may be single on this second showing.

Once established, large-flowered clematis can be vigorous and should be lightly pruned early in the year before the current growth starts. It is useful to understand about old and new growth in connection with pruning, since early, large-flowered cultivars can produce flowers on the previous year's shoots as well as on the current year's new shoots. In late-flowered cultivars, the flowers come from the current year's new shoots, so do not hesitate to prune back old, untidy stems.

Right: 'Gillian Blades' is an exceptionally fine, early, large-flowered, pure white cultivar, with crenulated edges. It can be grown in any position and only needs light pruning.

Right: 'Mrs Cholmondeley', another early cultivar, has large, somewhat floppy, lavender-blue flowers. It grows in any position, reaching about 16ft(5m), and only needs light pruning before bursting into life in spring.

Left: *A very popular, trouble-free, late-flowering cultivar is 'Rouge Cardinal', which produces a mass of crimson-red flowers in late summer and fall. They associate well with heathers.*

Left: *The great saucers of 'Lasurstern's' deep blue flowers with their cream stamens are eye-catching early in the season. It does best in a sunny position*

Above: *In a shady spot, the large flowers of 'Nelly Moser' create a wonderful display of pink and lilac. It is an early-flowering cultivar that thrives well on trellis and walls.*

Large-flowered clematis

Although most of the mid- and late-flowering large clematis can be grown in full sun, it is not always best to do so, because the sun fades the large flowers. It is a good idea, therefore, to grow these large-flowered cultivars in partial sun or shade, perhaps along the side of a house, or to intermingle them with other plants or even to encourage them to scramble through a shrub or tree. Quite a few of the large-flowered clematis produce flowers 3-6ft(1-2m) off the ground, making them agreeably conspicuous and most of them are capable of growing to 16ft(5m). The later large-flowered clematis, such as 'Comtesse de Bouchaud', 'Ernest Markham' and 'Perle d'Azur', can grow to 25ft(7.5m), but these are exceptional. The magnificent flowers need to be appreciated at close range, so the best places to show off these fabulous, large-flowered clematis are on pergolas and pillars, arches and arbors. For portable displays in tubs and containers, use the early-flowered cultivars, such as 'H.F. Young', 'Niobe' or 'Miss Bateman'. The buds of large-flowered clematis are very attractive in themselves; their subtle hues are a hint of things to come and there is the anticipation of seeing them unfurl their giant flowers. The combination of fat buds, large, beautifully colored blooms and attractive foliage gives this group of flowering plants a special place in the garden.

Left: The buds, followed by large, soft pink flowers of the late-flowering 'Comtesse de Bouchaud' make a fine display on a trellis. It grows in any position; prune it hard for best results.

Below: *'Twilight' blooms freely from the summer to the fall and grows to about 10ft(3m). Here it is supported on plastic trelliswork and arches. It is best pruned hard before spring growth.*

Above: Clematis jackmanii *is a great favorite and 'Superba' is an improved cultivar with broader sepals. It grows to 16ft(5m). Here it is seen above a bed of periwinkle.*

Above: *Sadly, the pale primrose yellow of the early-flowering clematis 'Yellow Queen' quickly fades to off-white, so enjoy the mass of color while it is at its best.*

Right: *A close inspection of the velvety flowers of 'Niobe' reveals all its magnificent details, including the yellow anthers. It is an early-flowered clematis, whose deep reds are hard to beat. 'Niobe' can also be used for ground cover.*

51

Planting a clematis against a wall

Clematis are very versatile and growing them against a wall is just one way to display their gorgeous flowers. If appropriate for the variety, choose a wall that faces the sun, as this helps the plant to grow and the flowers to look radiant. The heat reflected and retained by the bricks aids growth and promotes a more vigorous plant. Do not plant clematis too close to the base of a wall as this will cause the plant to dry out. The wall provides good support for clematis stems to climb, but they will still need some assistance. You could tie them to trellis, attach them to a loose netting support or to wires stretched between vine eyes (see page 21). It is the nature of the clematis plant to have seemingly dead stems lower down when it is mature and a burgeoning mass of foliage and flowers on top. On the wall, the natural growth habit of the clematis can be encouraged to suit your design needs, with either a great mass of plant high up or hanging down, or nicely arranged along the top of the wall, or arranged sideways across the wall. For the best effect, a trellis against a white wall not only helps to draw attention to the plant and its flowers, but also acts as a good support for the plants.

3 Remove the plant with its stake and place them in the prepared hole, so that the surface of the rootball is about 4in(7.5cm) below the surface.

4 Replace the soil carefully around the plant and firm it down with your knuckles. Take care not to break the delicate stem attached to the stake.

Soaking the plant

Before planting, plunge the plant in its original pot into a bucket of water and soak it for at least ten minutes so that the roots and rootlets are completely saturated.

1 Dig a hole about 12in(30cm) away from the wall and large enough to allow the plant to be positioned deeper than the soil level in its original pot.

2 Break up the sides and bottom of the hole and sprinkle in a handful of slow-release fertilizer to give the plant an extra boost of growth.

5 *Arrange the plant and flowers against the trellis. Leave the existing ties in place around the stem and cane, and tie in the rest of the plant so that it does not flop over.*

This is Clematis 'Voluceau', a late, large-flowering hybrid with petunia red blooms and contrasting yellow anthers.

6 *Apply a small amount of slow-release fertilizer around the base of the plant, but prevent it touching and possibly burning the stem.*

7 *Water the plant in thoroughly to help it become established. Do this every day for about a week, depending on the local conditions.*

Planting position

Be sure to plant the clematis sufficiently far away from the base of the wall to clear any dry spots or accumulated rubble. Remember that it needs space to establish itself. There is a good reason for planting the clematis at a deeper level than it was planted in its original pot. Should it be affected by clematis wilt or if the stems are damaged during weeding, the plant will be able to regenerate from the base.

Ultimate success depends on the planting position, a favorable aspect and suitable soil conditions.

Planting clematis in a tub

Clematis are great subjects for displaying in tubs and once in full bloom they make a wonderful centerpiece on a patio or porch. Although pots and tubs are available in a wide range of different shapes and sizes, it is fun to use white tubs, since these have a very refreshing look. The great advantage of white is that it is distinctive and so easily coordinated with the rest of your garden furniture. The square tub - or Versailles tub - is a throwback to the grand tubs that once contained oranges and bougainvillea. Every year they were hauled in and out of the orangeries according to the seasons. Today's humble version may follow tradition and be made of wood or be a plastic simulation. Being small, it is much more versatile for the modern garden and, charged with its colorful clematis, can be moved around the garden or patio for instant effect. Choosing the right sort of clematis for the tub is very much a matter of individual choice. It might depend on your color scheme or it might reflect some particular clematis that you are attracted to, perhaps one of the large-flowered varieties with a compact growth habit. These are the most suitable for a small tub and trellis as shown on these pages, and the pink *Clematis* 'Hagley Hybrid' meets all these criteria. Once the clematis has become established on its support, trim it regularly if you want the trellis and clematis to feature as a little vignette of color on the patio. However, if you want a vigorous plant to continue climbing, you can allow it to form a substantial plant up a wall or as a bower.

1 Fill the bottom third of the tub with a proprietory potting mixture that contains a balance of peat, grit, sand and possibly fertilizer. Make a hole in the mixture to accept the rootball.

Stand the pot in a bucket of water to soak the roots before planting.

2 Carefully remove the plant from its pot. Hold onto the cane, as the stem might break if it falls away. Ease the clematis with its cane into the tub.

3 Add potting mix to within about 2in(5cm) of the top of the tub and firm it down. About 2in(5cm) of the stem should be covered with the soil.

4 With the plant in position, you can begin to set up the first part of the pyramid trellis. Ease it in carefully at the back of the tub, working the legs into the container without disturbing the plant.

5 *Fit the next two sections of the pillar opposite each other and then work the legs into the potting mix, taking care not to damage the rootball. Follow the instructions.*

6 *Tie in any pieces of floppy vegetation to the trellis at regular intervals so that they are arranged as you wish, and to keep them away from the final stages of construction.*

7 *Ease in the final support without disturbing either the rest of it or the delicate stems or flower buds.*

Clematis 'Hagley Hybrid'

Clematis for containers

'Bees Jubilee'
'Comtesse de Bouchaud'
'Edith'
'H.F. Young'
'Hagley Hybrid'
'Horn of Plenty'
'Lady Londesborough'
'Lady Northcliffe'
'Lasurstern'
'Miss Bateman'
'Mrs. N. Thompson'
'Nelly Moser'
'Souvenir de Capitaine Thuilleaux'

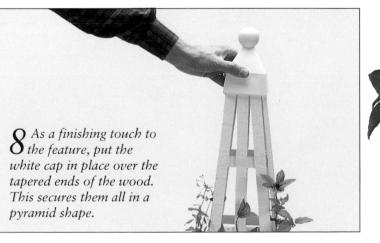

8 *As a finishing touch to the feature, put the white cap in place over the tapered ends of the wood. This secures them all in a pyramid shape.*

9 *Be sure to water the container profusely every day to ensure that the clematis becomes well established. Do not let it dry out at any stage.*

Taking clematis cuttings

1 *Select your cutting material from a good healthy plant and take it from the present year's growth. Make sure all your tools are razor sharp and have a plastic bag ready to put the cuttings in.*

2 *Place the shoot on a firm hard surface and, using a craft knife, cut the stem just above a pair of buds. The blade and the cutting surface must be scrupulously clean to avoid spreading disease.*

If you have a clematis that you really like, then you can grow identical plants from it, simply by taking stem cuttings. One long stem of the plant will yield several cuttings, but choose only the soft new growth produced in the current year. The best time to take successful cuttings is during the spring and early summer, when the fine weather will stimulate plant growth. You must be especially careful not to introduce diseases onto the cuttings, so it is a good idea to work with clean knives and secateurs on a clean surface. Remember that ideal conditions for plant growth are also good conditions for fungal attack. You can take the cuttings in the garden, but put them straight into plastic bags and seal the bags to ensure that the cut pieces do not wilt and lose too much water before you get them back to the house or greenhouse. Do not take cuttings during the hottest part of the day and do not leave the bags in the sun, otherwise they will suffer. Once you have taken the cuttings, pot them up as soon as possible. To begin with, you may find it easier to achieve success with cuttings from one of the more vigorous types of clematis, such as montanas. Once you have raised these, you can try take cuttings from some of the early summer hybrids that flower on the current season's growth.

3 *You can take a number of cuttings from one shoot, but be sure to use only the best sections. Be ruthless and discard all the thin, weak parts.*

These sections will make ideal cuttings, as they are firm and healthy pieces of the plant.

4 *If the section of stem between the leaf joints is very long, reduce it so that the cutting will eventually be at the right depth in the potting mixture.*

5 *To reduce any water loss from large-leaved cuttings, remove part or all of one leaf. If the cuttings are smaller, you can fit more in each pot.*

6 Dip the cutting into hormone rooting powder and insert it into a pot containing 50 percent peat and 50 percent grit. Do not add any fertilizer.

7 Cuttings root best when inserted around the edge of the pot. At this stage give them a thorough watering.

8 Cover the pot with a plastic bag to retain a humid atmosphere. Place the pot out of direct sunlight. The cuttings should root within three to four weeks and can then be potted up.

New growth from a bud in the leaf joint.

These roots have sprouted directly from the stem.

9 The amazing results of a cutting of 'The President' after about six weeks. New roots have burst forth and a healthy new shoot has arisen from the original cutting.

Below: Clematis 'The President' is a well-known and popular variety. It has deep purple coloring and flowers right through the summer until the fall.

Honeysuckles - elegant climbers

Honeysuckles make important statements in the garden. They fill up vertical spaces, ramble over unsightly structures and can be trained up pillars and posts. But perhaps the greatest virtue of honeysuckles lies in their ability to fill spaces and produce flowers that are not only usually scented, but also have unique shapes, typical only of honeysuckles. As climbing vines, they may need some support and assistance to reach their goal, but their effectiveness as bowers and scent producers is invaluable. Not that all honeysuckles have scent; some have sacrificed their scent for stunning good looks. There has been much hybridization of honeysuckles to increase the range of colors and forms. The largest honeysuckle of them all, *Lonicera hildebrandtiana*, has 6in(15cm)-long tubular flowers. It is a conservatory plant in Europe, but is grown outside over pergolas in the western United States. Some honeysuckles are evergreen or semi-evergreen, but this is often affected by latitude; the more northerly the location, the greater the chance that an evergreen honeysuckle will lose its leaves. Honeysuckles are not only good to look at, but they are important plants in any wildlife garden, as their berries are a useful source of food for a wide range of birds.

You can propagate honeysuckles either by taking stem cuttings in the summer or fall or by germinating seeds in spring or the fall. Pruning is normally restricted to thinning out overgrown and unruly plants after flowering. Many mature honeysuckles can be left just where they are during the winter months with minimal or no management.

Above: The orange throats of the two-tone flowers of Lonicera x heckrottii *justify its other name of 'Gold Flame'. Notice how the upper leaves are fused together.*

These flowers are borne in summer and pervade the garden with their scent.

Typical honeysuckle flowers are long, thin and tubular and borne in pairs close together.

Left: The coral, or trumpet vine, honeysuckle, Lonicera sempervirens, *is a hardy native vine of the east and south of the United States and was introduced to Europe in 1656. Its red-orange flowers with yellow throats are variable, as can be seen, but unfortunately they are scentless.*

Left: *Floral delights are on show here, with a great mass of the woodbine,* Lonicera periclymenum, *set against a field of 'Ladybird' poppies. Shakespeare used the term 'woodbine' to describe honeysuckle.*

Right: *The red flowers of the hybrid scarlet trumpet honeysuckle,* Lonicera *x* brownii *'Dropmore Scarlet', are attractive alongside the rounded green foliage. This semi-evergreen climber flowers in summer and fall.*

Honeysuckle berries

Honeysuckle flowers quickly turn into these clusters of berries, or fruits, containing seeds that ripen in the fall. Some species have more or less attractive berries than others; these particularly fine ones come from the flowers of L.p. 'Belgica'.

Right: *These are the stalkless flowers of* L. periclymenum *'Belgica'. They appear on bushy plants in early summer.*

Sweet honeysuckles

Below: Just like a cascading fuchsia, such as 'Thalia', this aptly named Lonicera x brownii *'Fuchsioides' is a picture of color on a red brick wall.*

Honeysuckles are grown mostly for their flowers and therefore have plenty of glamorous appeal. The range available for the small garden is overwhelming, and when making a choice you should consider not only the early- and late-flowering varieties, but also those with beautiful fruits in the fall, including *Lonicera nitida, L. pileata* and *L. tatarica,* with its red globular berries. In the newer hybrids there is a tendency for even larger flowers, and their colors may be quite striking or, in contrast, quite subtle. *Lonicera* x *tellmanniana,* for example, has gorgeous yellow blooms, but is unscented. It was created as a hybrid from a Chinese and an American honeysuckle. For the best scented honeysuckle, try *L. periclymenum* 'Serotina'. Honeysuckles make a great contribution to foliage, too, especially the variegated leaves of *Lonicera japonica* 'Aureoreticulata' or the thicket, hedgerow-like growth of *Lonicera nitida,* which has an attractive 'Baggesen's Gold' variety. Honeysuckles are easy to grow in most soils, as long as they do not become waterlogged. They can reach up to 30ft(9m) in height if given sufficient support. As native honeysuckles prosper in the dappled light of the understory of woods, it is not surprising to find that they make good subjects for shady gardens, but they can thrive in direct sun as well. Their scent and color are very attractive to insects, especially moths. Where honeysuckles are grown in tropical and subtropical American gardens, hummingbirds are frequent visitors, using their long tongues to reach the sweet nectar at the base of the tubular flowers. Altogether, honeysuckles are a very versatile group of plants.

Lonicera x americana *is best displayed on a pillar, since it is a medium-sized climber that does not reach the rooftops.*

Some choice honeysuckles

L. etrusca
L. fragrantissima
L. hildebrandtiana
L. japonica *'Halliana'*
L. maackii
L. nitida
L. periclymenum
L. p. *'Graham Thomas'*
L.p. *'Serotina'*
L. pileata
L. sempervirens
L. tatarica
L. *x* tellmanniana

Lonicera 'Serotina', with its beautiful reds and creams, is one of the so-called late-flowering Dutch honeysuckles.

The very pale cream-and-white honeysuckle, L. 'La Gasnérie'.

The very popular L. 'Graham Thomas' has a delightful mix of colors and large blooms.

Above: The beautiful apricot yellow flowers of L. x tellmanniana *make a good color match with the marjoram and poppies.*

Below: Honeysuckle drapes this cottage in summer. Thin out rampant growth each year, but do not lose the smothering effect.

Honeysuckle planted in a tub

Honeysuckles are universal favorites and there are many different species and cultivars to choose from. They can be grown in hedgerows, up trees, as pillars or as specimens in a tub with a trellis support. They are energetic stem climbers, have spectacular flowers and can fill the evening air with evocative scents. So which do you choose? There is a good chance that your native honeysuckle will perform the best in your area, but there are many others, such as *Lonicera periclymenum* or *L. etrusca* that you can grow as species of honeysuckles. Other good performers include *L.* x *americana*, 'Gold Flame' and the favorite, 'Graham Thomas' featured here. Honeysuckles can contribute to many yellow and green themes in the garden, whether they are grown in pots or not. You might consider Japanese honeysuckle, *Lonicera japonica* 'Aureoreticulata', or the yellow trumpet honeysuckle *L. sempervirens f. sulphurea*. In hotter areas with a typical Mediterranean climate, the Burmese honeysuckle, *Lonicera hildebrandtiana*, can look staggering with its 7in (18cm)-long yellow-orange giant flowers. This powerful climber is ideal for growing on pergolas, where it will relish the sunny conditions.

1 *Fill the tub with a suitable potting mixture and make a hole in the center large enough for the rootball to fit with ease, allowing about 2in(5cm) of soil below the roots.*

2 *Tap the nursery plant out of its pot, together with its cane, and place the rootball into the hole, taking care not to lose too much of the soil adhering to the roots. Firm it in well.*

3 *Add more potting mixture around the plant. Distribute the mixture evenly in the box and level it off to within 2in(5cm) of the top of the pot to allow space for watering.*

5 *Use soft string to tie individual climbing stems to the trellis, taking care not to damage any of the delicate stems. Tie the knots loosely.*

6 *Also use string to tie the cane to the trellis. Again, take care not to crush or damage the climbing stems of the plant.*

4 *Gently firm in the soil around the plant to eliminate air gaps, which would prevent the roots developing. Add more potting mix if necessary, but leave a space at the top.*

7 *Give the honeysuckle a generous watering to ensure that it gets off to a good start. Water it every day for ten days so that it becomes established and do not allow it to dry out after that.*

A stout pillar made from six canes secured at the top provides plenty of support for these sweet peas.

Sweet peas

Most of the sweet peas that we grow belong to one species, *Lathyrus odoratus*, a name that aptly describes its scented nature. However, this attractive wild pea has been the subject of a great deal of cross-breeding and now there many varieties to choose from. There are several other members of the *Lathyrus* genus and some are perennial, but the sweet pea is an annual. For best results, sow it in early fall, as seed sown in the spring will not produce the tallest plants. Sweet peas benefit from thorough soil preparation, which involves double-digging a trench and working in plenty of well-rotted manure. Soak the seeds before planting them to give them a better start. The plants will need staking to help them climb or you can tie them to canes or sticks arranged in the same way as for growing a row of tall peas. Sweet peas climb by using the long tendrils that arise at the base of the leaves. Being a member of the pea family, Leguminosae, they bear typical asymmetrical pea flowers with wide wings and a landing platform on which bees can alight when collecting nectar. It is the flower itself that has been improved in terms of its size, color and scent, which are the main virtues of the sweet pea. There are many different types of flowering pea and it is not hard to find one to suit your preference, be it an annual or biennial, spring- or summer-flowering type or one of the dwarf forms suitable for scrambling over the ground.

Above: The secret of the sweet pea's climbing success is clearly visible here. The lead tendril has four parts, each one ready to twist round a support. This is Lathyrus *'Annie Good'.*

Sweet pea varieties

'Alan Titchmarsh'
'Ballerina'
'Bicolor'
'Bijou'
'Galaxy'
'Jet Set'
'Knee-hi'
'Leamington'
'Little Sweetheart'
'Old Spice Mixed'
'Painted Lady'
'Swan Lake'

Left: The virtue of growing sweet peas in a pot is that they can be moved around the garden to create an instant effect. Here, a wigwam of sweet peas make an effective foil for other plants.

Right: A pyramid of wooden trellis panels makes a suitable structure for sweet peas to display themselves. The long tendrils reach out to find suitable purchase points.

Above: The 'Anniversary' sweet pea is white with a suspicion of pink at the tip of its petals, which have attractive wavy edges. It is a tall climbing plant with abundant flowers.

The everlasting sweet pea

The everlasting sweet pea, Lathyrus grandiflorus, *is a perennial much associated with cottage gardens. Once planted, perhaps against a wall, it consolidates its position and produces a huge root. This will sustain the 10ft(3m) of growth it can produce each year.*

Below: Once established, Lathyrus grandiflorus *produces a mound of hundreds of flowers.*

Climbers in combination

Many climbers climb up themselves by throwing off numerous shoots that twine around each other. Why not harness their vigorous enthusiasm by growing two or more climbers together? One very woody and sturdy species, such as a wisteria, can be used to support a more delicate species, such as a clematis, but the wisteria needs to be supported in the first place. Clematis are very obvious and easy choices for climbing through rambling roses or clumps of honeysuckle. The color of the combinations may be critical if you are seeking hues that harmonize with each other. For example, you might try *Wisteria* and *Clematis* 'Nelly Moser' - the pink clematis highlighting the purple of the wisteria flowers. The yellows in *Clematis* 'Bill Mackenzie' complement the yellow leaves of golden hop, while the scarlet of *Tropaeolum speciosum* tones with the maroon of *Akebia*. Virginia creepers go well with decorative climbing vines, all of which have fall colors, and hops thrive with ivies. The choice in warm Mediterranean climates is even greater, with the possibility of picking and mixing *Bougainvillea*, *Mandevilla*, *Cobaea*, *Campsis* and *Pyrostegia* in all sorts of jazzy combinations. In warm gardens where the aim is to create a conscious color scheme, perhaps all-yellow, all-white or all-red, you can give full reign to your imagination. Species such as the yellow butterfly vine, white *Stephanotis* and red *Passiflora* or *Ipomoea* can all become the basis for some spectacular displays.

Left: In summer, the fragrant honeysuckle, Lonicera periclymenum *'Graham Thomas' has white flowers that turn yellow with age. It blends well with the double flowers of* Rosa *'Handel', which are cream, but edged with a delicate shade of pink.*

Left: *Wisteria has plenty of foliage for most of the year and can be brightened up with another climber growing through it. Here, it is supporting* Clematis montana.

Below: *The deep pink sweet pea,* Lathyrus grandiflorus, *growing through the palest pink Rosa 'New Dawn' and the pink-purple Rosa 'Zéphirine Drouhin'.*

Above: *During the summer, honeysuckle with* Clematis 'Ville de Lyon' *growing through its midst creates a dense mass of flower and foliage against a brick wall.*

Below: *A delightful color-coordinated display is created here with Rosa 'Zéphirine Drouhin' and Clematis 'Richard Pennell' happily entwined together on trellis.*

67

Climbing potatoes

Most of the 1,700 species of *Solanum* are native to South America and amongst them are several climbers. The ordinary potato is a *Solanum* species, but it is not a climbing plant. However, it has plenty of near relatives that are climbers and these are conveniently called 'climbing potatoes'. Other relatives in the garden and hedgerow, such as eggplants (aubergines) and nightshades, are scrambling plants, but not quite climbers. Climbing potatoes produce clusters of flowers that vary from white and cream to purple and blue, and these are borne along the stem at regular intervals. While the stems of these scrambling and climbing plants may be supple or woody, some of them have tough spines to assist their advance forwards and upwards, so in the garden it is important to beware of these. Climbing potatoes can be grown in a tub, supported on a stake and trained up the side of a house. Alternatively, grow them at the back of an herbaceous border to scramble up a wall, where they contribute to seasonal foliage and color with their own pastel shades through the summer and into the fall. A number of species are commonly called potato vine, but this name is generally applied to the popular *Solanum jasminoides*.

Right: *The typical color of the star-shaped flowers of the potato vine,* Solanum jasminoides, *is bluish white, but this is the white-flowered form, 'Album'. It is a half-hardy evergreen.*

Left: *This shrubby climber is* Solanum wendlandii, *the paradise flower or giant potato vine. Although it has pleasing flowers, the stem is spiny. There is also a form with white flowers.*

Left: Solanum crispum 'Glasnevin' can climb to 20ft(6m). If planted at the side of a house, it will bush out and provide a rich display of green and purple flowers over a long period.

Above: Two climbers together vie for space; the golden hop, Humulus lupulus 'Aureus' provides leaf color, but Solanum crispum 'Glasnevin' is winning with its abundance of flowers.

Planting a climbing potato

Climbing potatoes make exciting subjects in pots or tubs for their flowers and foliage and are fun to grow. They twine with their stems, but usually need a little support by being tied to trellis. It is best to choose a fairly large tub and to buy a well-grown nursery plant, such as the *Solanum jasminoides*, or potato vine, a native of Brazil. The white form, *Solanum jasminoides* 'Album', is featured on these pages. Climbing potatoes are best situated out of direct drafts and in a spot where they receive plenty of sun. There are other species that enjoy long hot summers, so where the climate is suitable try the erect blue potato tree, *Solanum rantonnetii*. This evergreen shrub bears deep purple flowers through the summer months and although not strictly a climber, can be trained to cover a warm, sheltered wall.

1 Fill the pot to within about 4in (10cm) of the top with soil-based potting mixture. Trowel out sufficient soil to make a hole large enough to accommodate the rootball.

2 Soak the potted plant in water and allow it to drain. Tap it out of its pot, with its cane, and insert it into the soil so that the stem is covered by about 2in(5cm) of soil. Firm the plant in with your knuckles.

3 Having firmed down all round the edges of the planted climber, top up the tub with more potting mix to within about 2in(5cm) of the top of the pot. Firm down lightly once more.

4 Cut off some of the nursery ties, especially if they are too tight and restricting plant growth, but take care as you release the plant. Separate the various climbing stems.

5 You will need a few ties to attach the climbing stems to the trellis. Twist ties are the easiest to use, as they can be quickly put in place, adjusted or moved as the plant grows.

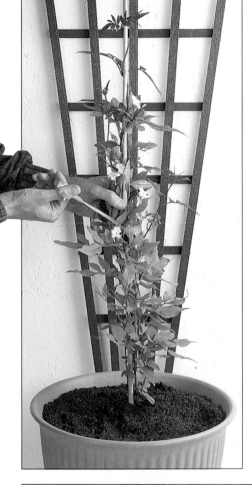

Tie in new growth as necessary. This Solanum jasminoides 'Album' can grow up to 20ft(6m).

6 Give the plant a good watering to encourage it to grow in the best possible conditions. Water it every day for about ten days and then check it regularly to make sure that it does not dry out.

7 The green trellis is a good contrast against the white wall and shows off the plant to advantage.

Climbers in shady places

Not all parts of the garden can be in sun all the time, and many gardens have dark corners between buildings or under trees, where the lack of light restricts growth. In these situations, it is best to plant species that are naturally tolerant of low light levels. If you want shade-tolerant and evergreen species, then choose ivies of the *Hedera* genus or *Euonymus fortunei*, which has attractive, bright yellow-and-green leaves, or some of the honeysuckles. There are other species that are shade-tolerant, but they have the disadvantage of being deciduous, such as the climbing hydrangea, *Hydrangea petiolaris*, and Boston ivies, *Parthenocissus*. If the plan is to cover a wall with a climber, then use *Parthenocissus* or *Hedera*, since climbing hydrangeas and *Euonymus* though very decorative on a small scale, cannot smother effectively. In the wild, many climbers have to scramble through dark thickets and scrub and are naturally inclined to thrive in shade; honeysuckles and hops are good examples. To brighten up the shade you could choose the yellow variety of hop, but do not expect shade-growing plants to do as well as they would in sunnier conditions. In shade, they tend to have longer gaps between leaves, fewer leaves and generally look a bit thin and less vigorous than normal. In time, however, it is possible to achieve good cover, which you can liven up by bringing in climbers in pots.

Right: All virginia creepers, Parthenocissus *spp., are ideal for growing in shade and do a fine job of concealing any unsightly structures, or just covering a bare wall where nothing else will grow. Although they lose their brightly-colored leaves in winter, they are not very destructive to masonry and so are excellent candidates for those shady places.

Above: Hops make good subjects for shady walls, although the foliage dies down in winter. The yellow form adds extra color in a shady area.

Right: A woodland wild flower extravaganza, with climbing hydrangea, hosta and foxgloves creating harmony in the shade.

Above: *Ivy normally thrives in deep shade and will perform well in the garden. There are many varieties to choose from, but opt for the darker green ones, as they are better adapted to live in shade than the more attractive yellow-leaved varieties, which lack the pigments necessary for life.*

Right: *Tropaeolum speciosum prefers to have its roots in the shade, but its foliage and bright scarlet flowers in sunshine.*

Lonicera japonica
'Aureoreticulata'

The young leaves of Actinidia
kolomikta *start off green but
then change to pink at their
tips. Actinidias, or kiwis, as
they are also known, need
support on which to climb.*

Foliage galore

There is nothing quite like employing effective foliage
plants to bring nature to your doorstep and if you choose
the right climbers, you can soon cover unsightly structures
or enclose a small garden to give it a special verdant touch. Fortunately,
there are a number of good performers, either for climbing up walls or
spilling over them. The advantage of gardening with strong leaf effects is
that colors and textures can be determined either seasonally or all
year round. Climbers that change their leaf color with the seasons
add an extra decorative dimension, such as the highly versatile
Virginia creepers, *Parthenocissus*, the large-leaved vine, *Vitis
coignetiae*, or the exciting pink-leaved kiwi, *Actinidia
kolomikta*. Alternatively, choose a golden variety of a
climber such as the golden hop, *Humulus lupulus* 'Aureus'.
Then there are the curious climbers, which are more leaf
than flower, such as the chocolate vine, *Akebia*. In
hotter areas, *Antigonon* will thrive or even some of
the tropical passion flowers, *Passiflora*. However,
most of these climbers lose their leaves in winter,
so if it is your intention to maintain a permanent
green foliage effect, then evergreens, such as the
ivies, *Hedera*, or golden honeysuckle, *Lonicera
japonica* 'Aureoreticulata', would be suitable for
temperate areas, or the small-leaved and clinging
creeping fig, *Ficus pumila*, for warm climates. In the right
conditions, the creeping fig
makes a superb smothering
climber on a wall. In fact, it is a
highly versatile plant, as it is also
suitable for hanging baskets, as well
as a good houseplant, especially
the variegated leaf form.

Left: *Given a good support, this
variegated honeysuckle,* Lonicera
japonica 'Aureoreticulata' *will
quickly cover the area with its
attractive leaves. It is mostly
or wholly evergreen.*

Humulus lupulus
(normal green form)

Humulus lupulus *'Aureus'*
(golden form)

Above: *Some of the curvaceous leaves on a mature bush of* Actinidia kolomikta *look as if they have been splashed with pink or white paint*

Right: *The golden hop,* Humulus lupulus *'Aureus', creates a striking effect when grown against the green form. Both are vigorous climbers.*

As the plant ages, the leaves close to the flowers take on a variegation of white and pink. The small white flowers are no match for the splendid mature leaves.

Right: *The trusses of flowers on the chocolate vine,* Akebia quinata, *hang down among the unusual five-lobed leaves that provide the main interest in this vigorous climber. The spring flowers carry the scent of vanilla.*

Left: The eye-catching leaves of Humulus lupulus 'Aureus' the golden hop, will smother walls, pillars and unsightly structures.

Pruning hops

Hops burst out of the ground in early spring with an unbelievable enthusiasm and thrust upwards and sideways with long, thin, twining stems. Each plant puts on a prodigious amount of vegetation during spring and summer and all of it must be cut back to ground level in the fall, otherwise you are left with a mass of withered and twisted brown stems that may harbor insects and fungal pests and diseases. The principle of pruning hard back to the base of the plant is essential for these plants, which are both perennial and deciduous.

The best way to propagate hops is to take cuttings from underground stems. It is the female flowers that are the commercial source of hops used in flavoring beer. The flowers are papery and membranous and quite unlike the sprays of male flowers. The plant is a native of southern Europe, but it has been introduced to many countries, where it has escaped and now grows wild in the countryside. The yellow-leaved form is a most attractive change from the usual dark green leaves.

1 *Towards the end of summer, just before they fall, hop leaves become damaged and unattractive. Cut back the plant to ground level, removing all the prolific aerial growth.*

2 *Start by cutting off one of the main stems about 2in(5cm) from the ground. To disengage the stem, cut off the side shoots that wrap themselves around other stems.*

Left: The three-lobed leaves of the hop are very clear in this photograph, as are the long, searching stems of another climber, a clematis (left).

Fan-trained hops

You can improve the capacity of hops to smother a surface effectively by putting in a series of strings that radiate out from the base of the plant. The numerous twining stems then twist their way along these paths and within two months will have completely covered the wall with their leaves.

Above: *Radiating strings in place.*

Right: *The hop has rapidly clothed the strings with dense green foliage.*

3 Cleanly cut away all the other stems, leaving short pieces above ground level so that you know where the plant is and do not damage it when working over the beds in winter.

Even after leaf fall, tiny shoots develop at the base of the plant - a sign of the following year's growth.

4 Label the plant clearly. Although the cut stems are visible now, the plant remains inactive underground for four months and may become covered with debris and weeds.

Preventing disease

Although they are exceedingly vigorous and prolific in leaf production, hops are susceptible to insect attack, which can stunt their overall growth and spoil the attractive leaves. Aphids and whitefly may attack leaves, so control them with a proprietary insecticide. The hard pruning that is essential for hops helps to eliminate the spread of disease. It is also a good idea to burn all prunings as a further precaution. The leaves of the hop are also eaten by the caterpillars of the comma butterfly, but they cause little damage. It is much better to encourage butterflies than to mourn the loss of a few leaves.

Virginia creepers for seasonal impact

Virginia creepers *(Parthenocissus* sp.) are great climbers and ideal for covering walls. They can smother buildings completely, producing wonderful fall colors of orange and red. They usually climb by means of tendrils with sticky disks or hooks at the end, but these do not damage masonry in the same way as ivy does. Most Virginia creepers need support to start with, especially *P. inserta,* which has no adhesive pads, but then they take over completely. Once established, they can be used to tumble as a curtain over walls, arbors and pergolas. All Virginia creepers - there are about 15 species - are deciduous, so you must be prepared for bare walls in winter and barrowloads of leaves to collect in the fall. The large leaves have interesting shapes, often with three or five lobes or leaflets, and the fruits, when present, are often like clusters of small blue berries.

During spring and summer, the green leaves are a useful foil for showing off other plants, or you could grow, say, climbing nasturtiums *(Tropaeolum)* through them. True Virginia creeper *(P. quinquefolia)* is a native of eastern North America, as is *P. inserta,* but most of the other Virginia creepers grown successfully as wall features worldwide originate from China and Japan.

Right: *The vivid fall colors of* Parthenocissus quinquefolia - *enhanced by frost - contrast with the dark greens of the ivies behind them in this typical situation for the true Virginia creeper.*

P. henryana *has five fairly rounded leaflets on each leaf and the fall colors pick out the veining in pale tints. Leaf colors can be more startling when the plant is not in full sun.*

Left: *The Chinese Virginia creeper,* Parthenocissus henryana, *is a vigorous self-clinging climber with forked tendrils. It is not entirely frost hardy.*

Below: *This Virginia creeper is sometimes still called* Ampelopsis *and has previously been placed with the* Vitis vines, *but it is in fact* Parthenocissus tricuspidata, *which describes the three lobes of the wide leaf. Once established, it is a vigorous, self-supporting climber.*

Right: *The uniform rows of these blood-red leaves of* P. tricuspidata *make a remarkable show in the fall, but they can all blow away in a single storm.*

Below: *The first autumnal tints are visible on this* P. tricuspidata, *also known as Boston ivy. It is growing alongside* Vitis coignetiae. *The ranks of leaves make an attractive foliage effect in the garden.*

Ivies in variety

Ivies contribute more to gardening with their leaves than their flowers. Foliage features and textures is what they excel at, being evergreen. Ivy might seem rather plain at first sight, but there are several hundred varieties available, with leaves that range in form and color from small to large, wavy-edged or crinkled, green, variegated and yellow. There are so many to choose from that planning a bold foliage feature or combinations with other plants is easy with ivies. They are good at covering walls or the sides of buildings, but keep an eye on them in case their adventitious roots make a mess of the masonry. As ivies grow neatly and tightly, they can also be clipped to various shapes, which is an advantage in Italianate-style gardens. Specimens in pots can be encouraged to climb a small pyramid of trellis. Trimming removes the flowers, which most people are happy to forfeit, but in some varieties the flowers are very small and actually add character to the plant.

Right: In bright sunshine, the pale green leaves of Hedera helix 'Buttercup' live up to their cultivar name and turn a lovely shade of butter yellow. This frost-hardy ivy will do well in a sunny corner.

Hedera
'Sagittifolia Variegata'

Hedera
hibernica

Hedera helix
'Glacier'

The variegated leaves of Hedera 'Goldheart' are very distinctive. Once established, this cultivar grows quickly and can reach a height of about 20ft(6m).

Be sure to cut out any growths that revert to plain green foliage.

Left: Hedera colchica 'Sulphur Heart'. Climbing ivy stems can be secured to the wall, as here, but adjust the ties every year because the stems swell as they grow.

Right: The wavy margin of the leaf is the key feature of Hedera helix 'Ivalace'. The glossy green, frost-hardy foliage is ideal for covering a low wall.

The crested margins of these pale green leaves give this ivy cultivar the apt name of 'Parsley Crested'. It may be listed as H. helix 'Cristata' at garden centers.

Below: Hedera helix 'Adam', with its yellow leaf margins, makes an exciting addition to any wall. This cultivar can be damaged by frost.

Hedera colchica 'Sulphur Heart' (also known as 'Paddy's Pride') has broad variegated leaves that hang loosely from vigorous stems. Ideal for clothing a large wall.

Using ivy in the garden

In the wild, ivy is such an undistinguished plant that it is sometimes surprising that it should be responsible for some of the best foliage and design features in the garden. Its remarkable feature is the way it clings to surfaces, smothering them in uniform leaves, and there are many ways in which you can take advantage of the various colors and leaf shapes. And many ivy cultivars can be used as ground cover. Several hundred varieties of ivy are known, but they all prefer alkaline soils. Being a woodland species means that ivies are excellent subjects for shade. Their flowers are also enormously attractive to insects and their evergreen leaves provide good shelter for hibernating insects. Ivies can be employed with great success to hide any unsightly garden structures. Use them informally in wilder types of garden or clip them regularly in more formal plantings to keep them within prescribed limits. Another feature of ivies is that they can be used for topiary, providing you have a framework over which it can grow and you trim the plants regularly to shape. This means that ivy can be used with great effect in small spaces and, if grown in pots, can be moved around to create different moods. Because ivies are comparatively vigorous, it does not take long for the topiary subjects to take shape.

Left: Two climbers together: ivy and wisteria. The ivy, with its overlapping leaves, has shinned up the brickwork in its usual unrestrained way.

Below: You need to tread lightly in this garden, where at least two kinds of ivy have colonized both the vertical and horizontal surfaces of the steps, alongside many other plants.

Below: The yellow edges and irregular yellow patches on the leaves distinguish this Hedera helix 'Marginata Major' from other varieties. Its flower buds are just waiting to burst open.

Below: *A stone frog exploits the vantage point at the top of this pillar of ivy, making it a choice example of garden design - simple and inexpensive to create and yet enormously effective as a focal point.*

Above: *Ivy takes on the geometric form of the surfaces over which it grows, as few other climbers can do. This ability gives ivy a distinct advantage over other climbers; in formal situations it can add considerably to the garden design, particularly if you use an alternating pattern of differently colored ivies.*

Dividing ivy

1 Knock the ivy out of its pot and carefully pull the plantlets apart, taking care not to damage the roots too much in the process. Replant them without delay.

When you buy a pot of ivy from a nursery or garden center, you will find that it is made up of several rooted cuttings that are easy to split and replant where you want them.

2 You can divide the original plant into ten or more separate rooted cuttings that you can plant in small groups to fill particular spaces.

Making the most of climbing foliage

A garden rich in different kinds of foliage, evergreen or deciduous, is always a great boost for general enjoyment. The colors and textures of foliage, plus the way that some climbing plants creep or cover walls with a prodigious array of differently shaped leaves, makes for a well-integrated, natural look. The walls around patios and at the back of conservatories are fine places to show off a variety of foliage climbers. Since town gardens are often overlooked by neighboring houses and even rural plots may be overshadowed by nearby trees, shade-loving climbing plants are a natural choice for walls and trellises. The fact that many shade-loving plants produce more leaves than flowers is a characteristic that helps the gardener in these situations. Thus, in many parts of the world, this vertical gardening has to take place in the shade of trees and on the walls of buildings, since there is nowhere else to garden. Choosing foliage for color, shape and texture should be your priority.

Right: Ampelopsis glandulosa *var.* brevipedunculata, *is grown for its leaves, resplendent in the fall with a mix of yellow and green, as well as berries. It is a vinelike climber.*

Above: This attractive member of the cucumber family, the tendril-climbing Thladiantha dubia, *embraces a bust with its pointed, heart-shaped leaves. Yellow flowers will follow later.*

Below: *This New England cottage is richly festooned with foliage climbers such as Virginia creeper and ivy. In the fall, the walls will be a blaze of reds and oranges.*

Right: *The creeping fig, Ficus pumila, makes an intricate display and looks particularly good here on a white wall. It will thrive outside in warm climates, but is sensitive to frost.*

Hanging baskets of fuchsias add contrasting touches of color.

Vigorous grape vines

Vines are naturally very vigorous and must be kept under control. However, there will always be some plants that do not perform well, perhaps because they are poorly bred or not well established. The main thing to remember is that vines are naturally drought-tolerant, but only when they are established. You can lose many plantings if you do not water them well during their first few weeks to encourage root growth. In the wild and in vineyards, some vines grow out of very rocky ground with minimal soil, but at least it is well-drained and hot. A newly bought plant should have a well-formed rootball or a good set of roots. Make sure that the planting hole is large enough and thoroughly fork over a generous amount of well-rotted manure at the bottom. Assuming you have planted a grafted vine along with a sturdy support, the seemingly lifeless stem will burst forth with exuberant growth that will eventually have to be contained. Regularly tie the main stems to a trellis or other support to keep up with the advancing growth, and cut back any stems growing in the wrong direction. At the end of the season, prune the vine thoroughly to strengthen the plant and prevent long shoots flapping in the wind. During the winter, work in well-rotted manure around the base of the plant to recharge the vine for the following year's growth. Growing a grape vine as an ornamental weeping standard is possible, but requires a great deal of hard work to keep it within bounds.

Make a clean cut just past the largest bud of the current season's growth.

Pruning vines

In winter, cut back shoots of new green growth to two or three buds on from old, woody growth. Make the cut at the largest bud, as this will produce the best growth in the following year. Use the same method to train a vine along a wire.

Left: *The deep red leaves of* Vitis vinifera *'Purpurea' turn a deep purple in the fall and often remain on the plant. The foliage is more interesting than the fruits - small blue berries.*

Right: *Vines have a thick, woody base and need a permanent, strong support to climb up. Ornamental vines, with stems thicker than an arm, can survive for 200 years, covering a huge area.*

Below: A well-established vine can be too vigorous for a small house. In summer, cut back long shoots that venture over the roof or windows and prune the vine to its support in winter.

Above: In the fall, the leaves of Vitis vinifera 'Brandt' become mottled. They start the summer deep green, but change to yellows and reds, as well as orange, crimson and pink.

Right: When the vine becomes heavy with fruit, loop some string once around the stem and secure it to the support. This prevents the fruit moving and becoming damaged.

Passion flowers

Passifloras, or passion flowers, offer gardeners a great deal, as they are excellent climbers and have beautiful flowers. The unique structure of the flower has religious significance throughout much of the world. In the Christian religion, the ten sepals and petals are said to represent the ten faithful Apostles, the threadlike growths symbolize the crown of thorns, the five stamens the five wounds of Christ and the three-part stigma the three nails. Of the 500 tropical and subtropical species, about 60 have edible fruits. Granadillas (*P. quadrangularis*), for example, are grown commercially for their fruit, but with their staggeringly beautiful blooms, they also make excellent garden subjects. Of the ten passion flower species native to North America, one - *P. incarnata*, the Maypop passion flower - is the state flower of Tennessee. Many passiflora species can be grown outdoors in temperate climates, including the most commonly grown species, *P. caerulea*, which bears elegant pale blue flowers. In winter, the aerial parts of passion flowers are killed by frost; so remove them ready for the new growth in spring. In a conservatory, some of the more vigorous passion flowers can rapidly take over all the available space. Outside, they are best used on trellis or trained against walls.

Left: Passiflora citrina *is a new introduction from the pine woods of Honduras, where hummingbirds pollinate the pale yellow blooms.*

Right: *The giant granadilla,* Passiflora quadrangularis, *has huge flowers and equally large juicy fruits. In temperate climates, grow this is a conservatory climber and control its rampant growth by keeping it in a container.*

Left: *The strident bright red of this bat-leaf passiflora,* P. coriacea, *is highly distinctive. The best way of keeping the vigorous growth of passion flowers under control is by pruning in spring and summer.*

Below: Passiflora caerulea *has delicate rings of blue or purple in its flowers. If grown in a conservatory, the flowers do not always set and produce fruits.*

Right: *During the summer months, the developing pink buds of* Passiflora x caeruleoracemosa, *produce these fabulous flowers.*

Mandevillas

Mandevillas, together with the allamandas to which they are closely related, originate from the rainforests of South America. With their bold colors and large trumpet flowers, these delightful plants can make an important contribution to gardens. The blooms often have throats of contrasting colors. Mandevillas, also known popularly as dipladenias, are twining vines and can be grown up a support such as a pillar, either as a permanent feature or in a tub that you can move around for maximum effect. Mandevillas are ideal for a conservatory in temperate climates. They are semi-hardy to hardy plants and can be moved outside during the summer like orange or lemon bushes. Their great advantage is that they tend to flower in profusion and hold their flowers for a long period. One of the most widely available is a hybrid called 'Alice du Pont', which has rich pink flowers (but, sadly, no scent), but there are plenty of other species and cultivars available. During the growing and flowering season, be sure to keep mandevillas well watered but well drained. In winter, however, they do not need so much water. In the fall, prune stems back to within 2in(5cm) of the current year's growth. To take cuttings, use small lateral shoots or pieces of stem with two leaves and pot them into a peat and sand mixture in summer.

Above: Some means of support is essential for young mandevillas. These railings outside a house in Dallas make a good fixture and display for the twining stems.

Right: The deep throat and tubular shape of mandevilla flowers is very appealing. This is 'Alice du Pont', an attractive and reliable evergreen climber that grows to 10ft(3m).

Left: Mandevilla splendens *typically has pink flowers with a yellow eye. These blooms appear during the late spring and early summer among glossy green leaves.*

Left: *The white floral tubes and the yellow eye make this Mandevilla boliviensis very appealing. This vigorous, evergreen, woody climber needs protection from frosts.*

Below: Mandevilla rosea *is ideal as a decorative plant in a living room or trained up a wire in a conservatory or greenhouse. Provide warm humid conditions for all mandevillas.*

Keep mandevillas well watered - but not waterlogged - and make sure they are planted in a very rich potting mixture.

Morning glories

Ipomoeas, or morning glories, are fun plants to work with. At least 500 species are known and they have exciting colors. You can grow them on trellis, on banks or as a portable arrangement in a container. A particularly popular way of displaying them is as a run of plants along a netting or chain link fence, so that they flower along the entire length, but this only works in a hot sunny location. Opening their large, tubular flowers with the first rays of the sun, the plants are at their best in the morning, hence their common name. By afternoon, they are furled up in tight bud. Among the wide selection of ipomoeas are many annuals and biennials. All are best propagated by sowing seeds, rather than by any form of vegetative reproduction. Similar-looking biennial or perennial species belong to another group of plants called *Ipomopsis*. The deep purple of their flowers is immensely attractive to insects, such as carpenter bees and bumble bees, which take away pollen in exchange for nectar. Although ipomoeas are attractive ornamentals in the garden, they have a close relative that is a troublesome pest, namely bindweed, or convolvulus, *Convolvulus arvensis*.

Below: *Large* Ipomoea *flowers are very attractive to insects, but do not last long, quickly shriveling up after pollination.*

92

Left: A trellis allows the twining stems of ipomoeas to work their way to the top. Ipomoea flowers are very variable and often have different color 'eyes' in the center of the flower.

Right: Ipomoea coccinea *has tubular red flowers that are very tight compared with those of other ipomoeas, and the foliage is divided into fanlike palm shapes.*

A bee searches for nectar deep inside a flower of Ipomoea purpurea.

Above: All that is needed to support ipomoeas, here 'Pearly Gates', is a stiff form of trellis, and the plants will twist and turn their way to the top, shooting off flowers as they mature.

Left: When growing successfully, ipomoeas tend to swamp everything with their curvaceous heart-shaped leaves and wide-eyed flowers, thus creating an effective green curtain.

93

Elegant jasmines

The evocative scent of jasmine filling the evening air is just one of the great advantages of growing this versatile and multicolored group of flowers. They are busy and energetic climbers, well-suited for displaying next to doorways, over arches or just for covering walls or cascading over balconies. Not all jasmines are true jasmines; the Confederate, or star, jasmine much planted in North America is *Trachelospermum jasminoides*. It is a native of North America, but there are plenty of relatives found in Asia, too. While the scented Confederate jasmine is a superb plant for growing over structures, where it reaches up to 20ft(6m), it can also be used as an effective ground cover plant. In fact, it is quite at home in any Mediterranean climate, such as the Rivieras of France or Italy or along the Californian coast, where it soaks up the hot sun. As a group, jasmines have masses of little flowers with a range of delicate color hues, from white and yellow to pinks and red, and these shades can be usefully incorporated into garden designs. The tiny white flowers are particularly effective when planted near night-lighting, which picks out their delicate tracery of stems and flowers. Although the fragrance from jasmines is exquisite, bear in mind that not all jasmines are perfumed and not all of them are evergreen, either.

If you have a balcony, it is a good idea to grow scented climbers, such as jasmine, below the structure so that their perfume wafts upwards in the still evening air. This was done to great effect with balconies on many a plantation garden in Mississippi and Louisiana.

Above: Unfortunately, the flowers of the aptly named primrose jasmine, Jasminum mesnyi, *are unscented. They are borne singly on the square stems of the plant in spring.*

Below: Here, Trachelospermum jasminoides *cascades effortlessly over the side of the stairs, while its tiny flowers hang in clusters like showers of tiny stars.*

Right: The evergreen *vine* Jasminum polyanthum *needs full sun to thrive. It is a woody climber that needs to be pruned back every year. Its scented flowers are borne on the plant in large numbers through summer to late fall.*

Below: Jasminum nudiflorum, or *winter jasmine, is deciduous and an excellent climber for cooler climates. Given support, it can smother walls quite easily and is useful for brightening up an early winter day.*

Below: Yellow jasmine, Jasminum humile 'Revolutum', *a native of western China, has large butter-yellow, fragrant flowers from spring until fall.*

Bougainvilleas

Above: B. *x* spectoglabra
*'Sanderiana' bears masses
of deep purple bracts
among small, dark green
leaves. It has a loose and
upright growth habit.*

Bougainvilleas are a group of decorative plants native to South America, to which the French navigator De Bougainville gave his name in the late eighteenth century. He and his sailors may well have contributed to spreading the plant around the South Seas. In the world of garden plants, bougainvilleas take some beating for the sheer brilliance of their colors, which range principally from mauve, through purple to reds. Its characteristic way of growing is to put out long stems that scramble over the supports. Adventurous specimens reach the top of their supports and then arch over, creating a very colorful display. Bougainvilleas are certainly at their best in full sun; their flowery bracts are always open to it and the hotter the better. In some tropical locations they appear to be in flower all year round. Not surprisingly, bougainvilleas are very sensitive to frost and can only be grown outside in frost-free areas. Elsewhere they need to be containerized and you can then move the pots inside or out according to the season. Being a successful woody climber, bougainvillea can be used to smother porches, pergolas and arches. As the mature stem is armed with spines, it has been used as a defensive hedgerow, albeit a highly colorful one.

*The palest pinks are seen
in the maturing bracts of
Bougainvillea 'Mahara
Pink', which start off a
brownish pink.*

In Bougainvillea 'Elizabeth' the bracts are a rich purple-pink, made more striking by the uniformity of color.

The shades of copper, red and magenta of this Bougainvillea 'Killie Campbell' create a fine spectacle.

Orange-brown bracts with cream centers are typical of this Bougainvillea 'Rainbow Gold'.

Right: As this close-up shows, the true flowers of Bougainvillea are the cream-colored parts in the center. The colorful 'petals' are not petals at all, but bracts, which remain 'in flower' for a very long time.

Sun-loving bougainvilleas

Bougainvillea is one of the signatures of the tropics - the typical red colors standing out as a statement of the joys of gardening in the heat of the sun. Its spectacular nature is reflected in its second species name, *spectabilis*. The plant has traveled the world, and is especially popular in all those places that have a hot Mediterranean or tropical climate. One of the great advantages of the plant is that it is hardly ever out of flower. In milder, temperate climates it does not grow as well outdoors, but can perform very well behind glass. For this reason, growing bougainvillea in a pot is a hangover from periods when this colorful plant joined the migration in and out of the orangery, alongside citrus, bananas and cycads.

Because of its brilliance, this plant is assured of a place in any small garden. As a small plant, bougainvilleas have great appeal; you can put them out onto the patio and move them about, as well as taking them in as a houseplant during the winter. Such a potted bougainvillea would not look out of place in a backyard Italianate garden.

The flowers that we all admire in a bougainvillea are not, in fact, flowers at all, but colorful bracts. The true flowers are at the center of the bracts and are the insignificant creamish parts. There is an astonishing number of cultivars of *Bougainvillea*, ranging from weeping forms to plants with variegated leaves, from white or pink to purple flowers, singles as well as doubles. Then there are orange and orange doubles. All need tying to a support.

Right: *A healthy nursery bougainvillea should be growing firmly in a generous pot, have a stout, undamaged stem (beware of the spines) and look well proportioned, with plenty of flowers. This fine cultivar is* Bougainvillea *'La Jolla'.*

Above: *Bougainvilleas will flourish in direct sunlight and mature specimens can effectively cover large surfaces, smothering them with terrific flowers.*

Bougainvillea 'Apple Blossom'. The white bracts have an occasional flush of pink. Medium growth habit.

This rich, deep red bougainvillea with dark leaves is 'Vera Blakeman'.

Bougainvillea 'Mahara Red' has large heads of stunning double flowers. It has a compact growth habit because it puts all its 'energy' into flowering.

This is a variegated leaf cultivar called Bougainvillea spectabilis 'Weeping Beauty'. It grows slowly and bears these lovely light purple bracts.

Above: Bougainvillea colors are enhanced by the strong sun; two color forms grown together make a dazzling display against the blue sky.

Right: The variation in color and growth habit among bougainvilleas is well shown in this small selection of the many cultivars available.

Taking cuttings from bougainvillea

1 *Select healthy, non-flowering shoots that are semi-ripe i.e. firm but still green. Cut these into sections bearing about seven leaves, making the cut just below a leaf joint.*

2 *Remove some of the lower leaves to reduce water loss while the cutting is forming roots. You can prepare the other portion of the stem in the same way.*

3 *If there are large leaves still remaining on the cutting, you can reduce the water loss still further by slicing them in half.*

Bougainvillea is such a prolific climber that you can take plenty of cuttings without endangering a well-established plant or spoiling its appearance. In any case, there are often so many wands of vegetation that it benefits from some annual pruning to keep it within limits. As a small pot plant raised under glass in temperate climates, it might be more difficult finding a suitable semi-ripe, non-flowering shoot as a starting point. Given suitably warm conditions, it is not difficult to raise cuttings using the technique shown on these pages. Once you succeed with one variety, you will be encouraged to take cuttings from some of the other breathtaking colors and forms. In temperate climates, bougainvilleas are often sold in nurseries trained around a wire hoop. When your cuttings have established, you can grow them in this decorative manner and your greenhouse can then play host to all sorts of colorful varieties.

4 *To help the cutting form roots, dip each one in water and then into some hormone rooting powder formulated for semi-ripe cuttings.*

An ideal mix is equal parts of pure coir, perlite and fine-grade composted bark.

5 Insert each cutting into peat pots of well-draining potting mixture. Make a hole in the mix first so that the rooting powder is not scraped off. Firm each cutting in.

Right: The cuttings shown on these pages have been taken from Bougainvillea 'Raspberry Ice' (also known as 'Tropic Rainbow'), a compact-growing cultivar with bright red bracts and variegated foliage.

6 Remember to label the pots clearly with the name of the plant and the date the cuttings were taken.

After about six weeks, roots should start to grow through the moist walls of the peat pot.

7 Keep the cuttings warm and moist in a heated propagator set at 60-70°F (15-21°C). They should take about six weeks to root. Discard any that are not showing signs of rooting by then.

101

Tropical climbers

All the species mentioned on these pages are frost-sensitive and will only succeed outdoors in warm climates. Most, but not all, will grow in conservatories. The kind of climate they like best is subtropical, tropical or Mediterranean, with long hot summers. They all like water, especially in summer, but need less in winter. Typical of climbing vines from the tropics, which is where they all come from, they are adventurous and vigorous, making great colorful statements on the front of buildings, on walls and over terraces. Once established, they occupy a large amount of space and create a great deal of foliage mixed with flowers. They can be grown very effectively with other climbers that intermingle and push out a variety of flowers at irregular intervals. If you live in a temperate climate you can always aspire to these tropical delights and experiment with them in large conservatories or greenhouses. The appropriately named parrot's bill, (*Clianthus puniceus*), is probably the best one to start with. It is half-hardy and will only succeed in warm sheltered spots in full sun. It is frost-sensitive and may have to be covered or brought in during the winter. The tropical colors of the rainforest can be yours in the conservatory.

Above: *The orange-red flowers of the cross vine, or trumpet flower,* Bignonia capreolata, *are an unusual color. It is a vigorous tendril climber.*

Above: *The parrot's bill,* Clianthus puniceus *'Red Cardinal', belongs to the pea family. This unusual, striking climber comes from New Zealand.*

Left: *The calico flower,* Aristolochia elegans, *and the coral vine,* Antigonon leptopus, *make a contrasting and attractive bower in this Florida garden.*

Right: *The Latin American butterfly vine,* Stigmaphyllum ciliatum, *derives its common name from the seeds, which have butterfly-like wings. It climbs up pillars using twining stems and is a popular choice for yellow-themed gardens, as here in New Orleans.*

Beaumontia grandiflora, *a native of tropical Asia, flourishes here on the French Riviera.*

Above: *The rich reds of this Mexican blood flower,* Distictis buccinatoria, *can only be achieved in warm Mediterranean-type climates. It needs plenty of water in summer and full sun. Here it is growing with wisteria.*

Right: *The splendid herald's trumpet,* Beaumontia grandiflora, *is a vigorous woody vine that needs rich soil and a warm climate to flourish. It will not perform well in a pot. The large trumpet flowers are fragrant.*

Conservatory climbers

A conservatory is essential if you wish to grow tropical or subtropical climbers in temperate climates. Without this protection, non-hardy species, such as *Bougainvillea, Beaumontia, Stephanotis* and some of the thunbergias, as well as unusual climbers, such as the spectacular gloriosa vines, will die in temperate climates during the winter. It is not unusual for people to grow passion flowers or grape vines in a conservatory, but it is not entirely necessary in temperate climes, as they may grow so enthusiastically in a greenhouse that they cause a space problem. The best way to grow a grape vine in the conservatory is to plant it outside and to unleash all its growth entirely inside. Black-eyed Susan vines, or *Thunbergia alata*, make excellent conservatory plants with their creamy, white, yellow or orange colors and rounded leaves, but do not confuse them with black-eyed Susan, or *Rudbeckia alata*, which is an herbaceous perennial. There are at least 100 species of *Thunbergia* to choose from; another favorite is *T. grandiflora* which, like all the thunbergias, is a native of South Africa and Madagascar. It has blue flowers, hence its common names of sky vine, blue sky vine and blue trumpet vine. All these thunbergias are best grown as annuals and encouraged to climb up arbors, trellises, and over porches.

Above: Gloriosa rothschildiana *has superb red petals with wavy yellow edges. The plant can cover a well-lighted wall, with flowers appearing regularly from the foliage.*

Right: *Madagascar jasmine* (Stephanotis floribunda) *has very elliptical leaves and fragrant, white, waxy flowers that last a long time. It will twine up trellis in a conservatory and also makes a good houseplant.*

Left: *The bleeding heart vine, (Clerodendrum thomsoniae) is a twining evergreen shrub from tropical Africa. Its interesting white and crimson flowers are ideally displayed on a trellis - inside in temperate climes.*

Right: *The Australian, late winter-flowering bower plant (Pandorea jasminoides) has white flowers with pink throats, but there are all-white and pink cultivars, as shown here.*

Above: *The commonest species of Thunbergia climbers have yellow or blue flowers. This T. grandiflora has trusses of large, pale lilac-blue flowers. A white cultivar is known.*

Right: *Setting the mood (and scent) in this conservatory is a jasmine arch over a trompe l'oeil depicting a classic urn and pedestal, with the stylish addition of green garden furniture.*

Index to Plants

Credits

The majority of the photographs featured in this book have been taken by Neil Sutherland and are © Colour Library Books. The publishers wish to thank the following photographers for providing additional photographs, credited here by page number and position on the page, i.e. (B)Bottom, (T)Top, (C)Center, (BL)Bottom left, etc.

Gillian Beckett: 105(TC)
Eric Crichton: Copyright page, 13(BR), 22(L), 26(BL,BR), 31(L,TR,BR), 34(R), 35(R), 36-37(B), 38(TL), 39(BL), 42(L), 43(TL,B), 46(BR), 50(L), 51(TC,TR), 59(TL), 60(L), 61(TR), 66(L), 67(L), 69(R), 73(L), 77(TL), 82(BR), 83(TL), 84(L), 88(R), 90(BL), 93(BL), 95(TR,BC), 102(TR), 105(L)
Forest Fencing: 29(R)
Garden Matters/Jeremy Hoare: 98-99(C)
Garden Matters/John Feltwell: 22(B), 33(BL), 34(BL), 36(L), 38(B), 40(TL,B,R), 42(R), 44(R) 45(BR), 46(L), 47(CR,BR), 49(R), 59(TR), 64(R), 65(C,BR), 74(BC), 75(BR), 77(TC,CR), 79(L,BR), 82(L), 83(R), 85(B,TR), 86(BR), 87(L), 90(TR), 93(TL), 94-95(C), 98(BC), 102(L), 103(TL,TR,B)
Garden Picture Library/Steven Wooster: 105(BR)
John Glover: 12(BC), 13(TC), 22-23(TC), 23(TR), 29(TL), 37(TL), 41(BC), 43(TC), 45(TR), 61(BR), 66(R) 67(TR), 68(L), 72(L,R), 73(TR,BR), 75(TC), 78(T), 79(TR), 80(B), 81(TL,TR,BR), 86(L), 87(TR), 89(TL,BL), 91(TL), 92(R), 94(L), 95(BR), 96(TL), 102(CR), 104(T)
Andrew Lawson: 84(R)
S & O Mathews Photography: 12(TR), 30(TR), 44(T), 64(L), 82(BC), 93(TR)
Clive Nichols: Half-title page, 10, 13(TR), 21(BR), 23(BL,BR), 30(L), 37(TR,BR), 41(L), 44(L), 45(L), 46-47(T), 47(T), 50-51(C), 51(BR), 65(L,TR), 76(TL), 78(B)
Photos Horticultural: 35(L), 67(BR), 104(B)

Acknowledgments

The publishers would like to thank the following people and organizations for their help during the preparation of this book: Fred Godfrey of Sussex Plants Ltd, East Sussex; Forest Fencing Ltd, Worcester; Reads Nursery, Norfolk; J. Bradshaw and Son, Busheyfield Nursery, Kent; The Honeysuckle Group, Wiltshire; Long Man Gardens, East Sussex; Murrells Nursery, West Sussex; Kath and Alan Goode; Mike Lawrence.